THE UNITED NATIONS
SACRED DRAMA

Dedication of the text

For DONAL and RITA
FEDELMA and KATHLEEN
in the spirit of the Preamble

Dedication of the drawings

For CONOR
who initiated the venture

THE UNITE[D]
SACRED D[...]
CONOR CRUISE[...]
AND FELIKS TO[...]
SIMON AND SC[...]

NATIONS
RAMA
O'BRIEN
OLSKI
USTER

All rights reserved
including the right of reproduction
in whole or in part in any form
Text Copyright © 1968 by Conor Cruise O'Brien
Drawings Copyright © 1968 by Feliks Topolski
Appendix Copyright © 1968 by David Brokensha
Published by Simon and Schuster
Rockefeller Center, 630 Fifth Avenue
New York, New York 10020

First printing

Library of Congress Catalog Card Number: 68-24051

Designed by Michael Brett

Set in Monotype Plantin and
Printed in Great Britain by
Brightype Litho at
Taylor Garnett Evans & Co. Ltd.
Watford, Herts

CONTENTS

Text
9 to 33

Drawings: 1946–1961
34 to 47

Text
48 to 77

Drawings: In Action
78 to 115

Text
116 to 139

Drawings: In Session
140 to 221

Text
222 to 253

Drawings: Unanswered Questions
254 to 273

Text
274 to 300

APPENDIX
The Leopard-Skin Priest
David Brokensha
301 to 308

Postscript to Appendix
Conor Cruise O'Brien
309

Bibliography to text
311 to 317

Bibliography to Appendix
318

Acknowledgements
319-320

1

WHY, MEN often ask, does the United Nations not *act*? The answer is that it seldom does anything else: it is acting all the time. Almost all action, of course, involves an element of acting, in the theatrical sense; sociologists remind us of the number of *roles* we all play in our daily domestic, social and professional lives. National politics also, whether democratic or authoritarian in form, has always required play-acting, symbolism and ritual. Monarchy and drama were shoots from the same root; the fall of monarchy was seen immediately as, above all, a great curtain:

> *That thence the Royal actor borne*
> *The tragic scaffold might adorn*
> *While round the armed bands*
> *Did clap their bloody hands.*

The great statesmen who led the coalition from which the present United Nations grew were also no mean actors within their different cultural traditions: Gothic, Byzantine and Hollywood. In national States, however, there is a focus of real power, which limits what one might call the *role* of the *role*. If Stalin rose by mastery in dissimulation, and Roosevelt and Churchill by symbolising—that is to say by acting out—in the one case the will to beat the Depression, and in the other the will to beat the Nazis, they also had to take practical and binding decisions, both during their rise to supreme office, and after their attainment of it; they were actors not only in the histrionic sense, though they were that, but also and chiefly in the sense of being men who did things, who had and used real power.

It is different with the international entity which they created. It has no power except the actor's power:[1] the power to move, emotionally and morally. It has no *role* except a *role;* it plays the part of what men take it for. Its Council Chambers and Assembly Hall are stage sets for a continuous dramatisation of world history.

The United Nations is an imaginative creation, deliberately designed from its beginnings—in the Atlantic Charter, the Washington and Moscow Declarations, and the unveiling of the Charter in the San Francisco Opera House—to appeal to the imagination of mankind. The present essay is based on the supposition that it may be useful to approach this imaginative work as we approach others of the same kind: that is to say with the realisation that its truths are not literal truths, and its power not a material power. If this be granted, it follows that style and gesture, and even décor, may be more significant than

---

[1] The material power wielded in local peace-keeping operations is only an apparent exception (see pp. 134–9 and 222–7 below). The kind of material power envisaged in Chapter VII of the Charter never came to being: see p. 122 below.

the analysis of 'voting patterns', and the impact of a scene or a personage more significant than the letter of the Charter. Since the United Nations makes its impression on the imagination of mankind through a spectacle presented in an auditorium with confrontations of opposing personages, it may be said to belong to the category of *drama*. Since the personages, individually or collectively, symbolise mighty forces, since the audience is mankind and the theme the destiny of man, the drama may rightly be called *sacred*. I use the word as implying association, not with a supernatural order, but with those human needs which address themselves to such an order: the needs which create prayer, ritual and holy symbols. The origin of the United Nations drama is essentially the same as that of all sacred drama, in fear and in prayer. In the ancient drama the fear was of the gods, and the prayer was addressed to the gods. In this modern drama, man's fear is of man, and his prayer addressed to man. But the burden of the prayer—the aversion of a doom—is as it was of old, as appears from the famous opening words of the Preamble to the Charter:

'We the Peoples of the United Nations
Determined

to save succeeding generations from the scourge of war, which twice in our lifetime has brought untold sorrow to mankind . . . '

In their literal meanings these words are untrue. 'We' were not the peoples, but Roosevelt (and later Truman), Churchill and Stalin; the nations were not really united—as General de Gaulle was later to emphasise—and the peoples, so far from being 'determined', were not even consulted. But literal truth is irrelevant here: this is an invocation, the initiation of a series of solemn acts, designed to propitiate and purify. It is also the prelude to the creation of institutions symbolic of the prayer for peace, and dedicated to the continued offering of that prayer: the Security Council, the General Assembly, the Secretariat. Nor could there be any doubt that throughout the war-stricken world, those in whose name the prayer was offered would say, in some form, Amen. The fact of its being offered in their name was in itself significant. Older treaties—including the Covenant of the League of Nations—had been signed—in the traditional diplomatic style of 'the ancient cultures of contempt'—on behalf of 'high contracting parties'. The Charter—inspired by the Constitution of the United States—claims to speak on behalf of the people, and is in reality addressed to them, in terms of their known hopes and fears.

'The [San Francisco] Conference,' writes Professor Inis L.

Claude, 'was concluded in an unprecedented glare of publicity, and under the pressure of popular demand for a vigorous attack upon the evils of international life. . . . The articulate public willed the end but it did not with equal clarity will the means, and it may have been better satisfied with the drafting of glowing phrases than it would have been by the adoption of provisions essential to the genuine effectuation of the ideals which it espoused.'[2] The 'satisfaction' derived from the public offering of the 'glowing phrases' was in fact the same as that derived by the faithful from the public offering of a prayer: the sense of common aspiration; the appeal to a higher power, symbolised in this case by the Security Council and the General Assembly; the implied promise to meet again in continued acts of faith; the feeling that the thing feared may be averted, and the thing hoped for be won, by the solemn and collective use of appropriate words. This prayer still converges on the United Nations —as on a holy place—at times when, as in the Cuban missile crisis in 1962, or the Middle Eastern crisis of the summer of 1967, the scourge of war seems once more to be about to descend. It is the prayer that makes the drama sacred.

To speak of sacred drama is not to suggest that the United Nations dwells perpetually on some pure and solemn height: far from it. This drama swings from tragedy to farce and back again, neither bathos nor buffoonery is alien to it: all the unities, in every sense, are broken. As befits an institution which, as the French complain, is dominated by the Anglo-Saxons and is English in language (for most purposes) and style, the dramatic principles are more like Shakespeare's than Racine's. But we must imagine scenes from Shakespeare performed in no coherent order by a motley cast, most of whom have forgotten most of their lines and mangle the remains of what they remember. The actors almost always fall below, sometimes far below, the heights of the argument.

They are, most of them, actors such as angered Yeats:

> *But actors lacking music*
> *Do most excite our spleen*
> *They say it is more human*
> *To shuffle grunt and groan*
> *Not knowing what unearthly stuff*
> *Rounds a mighty scene.*

The scene remains mighty, even if the actors are not. The East River Shakespeare is a Shakespeare of the theatre of the absurd, suffused by nightmare in its form as well as in its

---

[2] *Swords into Plowshares: The Problems and Progress of International Organisation:* Third ed. pp. 57–8.

content. On its common level it is a desperately serious farce, on whose continued run our lives may depend.

The drama is of an extremely complex kind, nor is it at its least subtle when it appears to be most melodramatic and even 'corny', as in the great dual crisis over Suez and Hungary, in October–November, 1956. On that occasion Virtue and Hope were seen and heard to intercede with the Wicked Uncles; fascinated by the spectacle, men forgot that the Wicked Uncles were permanent members of the Security Council and also capable of speaking with the voices of Virtue and Hope. In the case of Suez, two of the Uncles, getting past the age for success in wickedness, were forced by their stronger brothers to disgorge. The ceremony of restitution was enacted in the General Assembly in a sort of Transformation Scene[3] which would have been regarded as a triumph for the United Nations, had not the real powerlessness of the organisation—in any but the moral, emotional and ritual senses of 'power'—been simultaneously and puzzlingly demonstrated in the case of Hungary.

'Soviet Union defies United Nations', read the headlines. In actual fact it was indifference, not defiance; none knew better than the rulers of the Soviet Union that the United Nations possessed no force that needed to be defied. What interested the rulers of the Soviet Union was not the attitude of the United Nations; it was the attitude of the United States, which alone possessed the force for counter-intervention. Whether the United States decided to intervene or not, it would be likely to use the stage of the United Nations for an appropriate representation of its chosen policy. It is true that—because of Article 27, requiring the concurring votes of the permanent members—it would be impossible to make intervention against the Soviet Union (or the United States, the United Kingdom, France or 'China') into a United Nations 'action' within the terms of Chapter VII of the Charter. This, however, was of much less significance than the subsequent clamour about 'the veto' would suggest. The fact was that all the United Nations could provide was a symbolic moral cover, a flag and a stage, and for these to work, strict legality—though useful if available—was not absolutely necessary. If the United States decided to meet the Soviet action with force it could get the General Assembly to

[3] Curiously, the idea of the dramatic use of the United Nations had originally occurred to the British Government in *preparation* for Suez. According to Anthony Nutting, Mr. Selwyn Lloyd, then Foreign Secretary, agreed, after Nasser's nationalisation of the Suez Canal, to use an appeal to the Security Council to '*set the stage*' for future action. The 'powerlessness of the United Nations' provided a pretext for unilateral intervention. At a later stage, when things had gone awry, a dramatic ritual of 'United Nations action'—in the shape of the Expeditionary Force—provided a pretext for dignifying withdrawal. As Jean Genet remarks in *Our Lady Of The Flowers:* 'Every premeditated murder is always regulated by a preparatory ceremonial and is always followed by a propitiatory ceremonial.'

endorse its action—as it had done in relation to Korea under the 'Uniting for Peace' resolution of 1950; the United States could in 1956 probably still count on the support of a two-thirds majority in the Assembly on any important issue.[4] It is true that, under the Charter, the Assembly has no role in such matters; but this, being a legal and not a dramatic distinction, has little relevance to the real functioning of the United Nations (see below, p. 128). Almost all Americans (and such of their allies as were interested in such things) would regard an 'intervention vote' in the Assembly as constituting 'moral warrant', within the spirit if not the letter of the Charter, and the legalistic objections of the Soviet Union and its allies would be no more than an addition to the propaganda armoury of that side. And not necessarily a useful addition; perhaps even a 'boomerang'. The Afro-Asian neutrals, to whom such propaganda would be addressed, dislike the 'veto'. They also regard the Assembly as more important than the Council, because in the Council the Charter allows them only minor parts, reserving the leading ones for the greater powers. The Afro-Asians therefore tend to think that Assembly resolutions should be, or perhaps in some sense already are, United Nations decisions. Since what a significant number of members think is in the Charter, or even think ought to be there, is often more important than what actually is there, an illegal manœuvre, widely supported, may be for practical—that is to say, symbolic—purposes just as valid 'United Nations action' as would be an action firmly based on the Charter. Thus the substance—a United States decision to intervene—would have been accompanied by a play of shadows, in the form of United Nations resolutions, flags and berets—as in Korea.

In fact the United States decided *not* to intervene. This decision also required a play, based not on Retribution but on Pathos. Legality, which would have been hustled into the wings if the United States had judged intervention opportune, now held the centre of the stage. The spectacle of *The Security Council Paralysed by the Soviet Veto* was followed by that of *The General Assembly Justly Indignant but Powerless to Act*. The spectators forgot, and were invited to forget, that neither the Security Council nor the Assembly ever had the power to act—in the sense of being able to enforce decisions—and that all that was actually happening was that the one country with the

---

[4] It has been argued that the two-thirds majority was not available. I believe myself that it could have been obtained—with many abstentions—if the effort had been made by the United States which it was not. In any case a bare majority, combined with the citation of Article 51 of the Charter—which allows the right of 'collective self-defence' when the Security Council is deadlocked—would have provided adequate 'moral warrant' if the United States had decided to intervene.

physical power to intervene in such circumstances was refraining from asking the Assembly for a rite legitimising intervention, but was asking instead for verbal condemnation—that is to say for a rite of purification through anathema, and not for a blessing on action. If the Soviet Delegation seemed to endure the subsequent commination services with a certain stolidity, this may have been in part because Soviet diplomats are naturally gifted in that direction, and accustomed to such verbal ill-treatment, and in part because their particular stage-directions call for such a manner: men who understand the laws of history are supposed to be calm in confronting the hysteria of those whom these laws have doomed irrevocably. But their stolidity probably also concealed a certain relief that those who had promised to 'roll back the Iron Curtain' chose to raise a curtain of a less formidable kind and to use the stage machinery of the United Nations as a substitute for action.

In the difficult circumstances, it was a remarkably successful presentation. The advance publicity, starring the author of *Crusade in Europe*, had prepared the audience for a drama of liberation. What they saw was a drama of enchantment. The hero still burned to liberate the lady, but he was bound and incapacitated in some mysterious way. Perseus had been announced; the scene disclosed the Fisher King. A chorus of diversely-costumed gnomes explained the plot in one sort of language from the podium of the Assembly; another chorus, of American editors and news-commentators, explained in different language, in the press and on radio and television. The second chorus was at least equally important, for it is in America that the stage is set and most of the lines are written. The general impression was confused but five messages came through, three of them clearly and two of them ambiguously:

1. The United States could do nothing to help Hungary;
2. This was not the fault of the Government of the United States;
3. To help Hungary was the responsibility of the United Nations;
4. The United Nations either could not or would not help Hungary;
5. This might or might not be the fault of the United Nations.

The audience on the whole, though bemusedly, accepted the main themes; it had, of course, extra-dramatic reasons for doing so; by this time the Soviet Union already had thermo-nuclear weapons and the American people, being saner than is commonly supposed, preferred 'to abandon Hungary' than to risk war in such conditions. The drama was a moral comfort; the guilt was shifted on to other shoulders. The terms of the shifting varied. Liberals and moderate conservatives expressed concern over 'the double standard' of the U.N.—a confused way of referring to the fact that the Soviet Union, in the area bordering on its own territory, was strong enough to resist the pressure of the United States, while Britain and France were not strong enough to resist the combined pressure of the United States and the Soviet Union on a Middle Eastern question. As far as the United Nations was concerned, necessarily remaining within the rhetorical and symbolic role which alone it is equipped to sustain, it did indeed apply a double standard—reflecting the balance of the forces dictating its rhetoric at that time—by formally 'condemning' the Soviet Union and refusing to condemn Britain and France. This, of course, was the opposite of the 'double standard' which its American, British and French critics imputed to it: such confusion seems inseparable from the discussion of the United Nations, and may—if the thesis argued here is correct—be inseparable from the nature of the United Nations itself.

Moderates, then, complained gently about the double standard and spoke about the need for Charter revision and the 'strengthening' of the United Nations. On this subject their language was necessarily vague, because the 'strengthening' they meant was at the expense of the Soviet Union, without whose consent the Charter cannot be revised. Articles 108 and 109 of the Charter provide that amendments and alterations to the Charter cannot come into force or take effect unless ratified by 'all the permanent members of the Security Council'. Soviet consent for the weakening of its own position seems inherently improbable. There is always a good reason for nonsense, and the good reason for this particular nonsense about Charter revision was that those who propounded it wanted to accept the standing excuse provided by the United Nations for American inaction over Hungary (and also over anything else in the future about which it might be expedient but inglorious for America to be inactive) and while they necessarily deplored this 'failure of the U.N.', and would deplore other failures, they *also* wanted to be in favour of the United Nations which many voters, especially middle-class women, identify with virtue. The solution for the dilemma is to deplore the *weakness* of the United Nations. In that way one is not merely in favour of the United Nations, but more in favour of the United Nations than other people, while not incurring any of the odium for those necessary 'failures of the U.N.' which are in fact, as practical politicians know, among the main sources of its usefulness, and especially of its real contributions to world peace. Logically those who speak of 'strengthening' the United Nations are on shaky ground. In terms of political rhetoric they are in a strong position; they hold the centre of the board. Since the United Nations that they defend is a purely Platonic one, by hypothesis purged of all the real and imaginary defects of that which exists in the world of phenomena, their stronghold in fantasy is inexpugnable. The real United Nations is already unreal enough, but both in its realities and unrealities it is steeped in the transcendent light of this other United Nations which the faithful discern above, around and before it, and which is the City of God.

For the extreme Right, however, it is precisely the absence of God which distinguishes the United Nations. 'God will be with us,' according to Senator Jack B. Tenney, 'because He never attended a session of the United Nations.'[5] Another Senator-theologian, William Knowland, reminded his fellow Americans of the relevance to the United Nations of a passage in Second Corinthians: 'Be ye not unequally yoked together with unbelievers: For what fellowship has righteousness with unrighteousness and what communion has light with darkness?'[6] For him, the Charter, with 'the Soviet veto', was 'a spider web' in which the United States was 'tragically enmeshed', the fated prey of 'that Godless communist totalitarian dictatorship'.[7] This doctrine, propounded at Georgetown University in February 1957, implies acceptance of the American administration theory that it could not act in Hungary because of the Charter and 'the Veto'—a theory which lacks all foundation because, assuming the Security Council to be deadlocked, the United States remained free to invoke 'collective self-defence'.[8] It is interesting—and even reassuring, in a macabre way—that the American Right adopted this myth. Senator Knowland is certainly astute and experienced enough to know that the United States would have acted in Hungary if it had judged it expedient to do so. In accepting the 'hands tied by the United Nations' theory, he and his friends were tacitly accepting the administration's decision on non-intervention; at the same time—by the acceptance of the 'bound by the Charter' myth—the unity of the Republican Party was preserved, and the folly of the Democrats, and the diabolical malevolence of their communist associates, were more firmly established. For who, after all, wrote the Charter? The Honorable Alvin N. Owsley of Dallas, Texas, has an answer which has commended itself to the whole of the far Right:

'The United Nations Charter was the work of Alger Hiss and his Communist, Socialist workers, beginning at Dumbarton

---

[5] *The United Nations: The Continuing Debate*, p. 17.
[6] *Continuing Debate*, p. 32.
[7] Ibid.
[8] Article 51.

Oaks; rewritten at Moscow, Russia (of all places!) and signed at San Francisco.'[9]

To the ambiguous spectacle on Turtle Bay, the far Right instinctively responds in terms of magic and melodrama. Alger Hiss prepares the insidious potion of the Charter, spiked with its paralysing Veto; Franklin D. Roosevelt commends the poisoned chalice to America's unsuspecting lips. Henceforward, until the spell be broken, America is confined within the chalk circle of the United Nations, while Communism's evil agents roam undetected from Kerala to California.

In the land which houses the United Nations, and which does most both to support and to use it, discussion of the functioning of the United Nations is almost all on this quasi-supernatural plane, whether it be in terms of the 'strengthened' Platonic U.N., or in terms of a U.N. of evil enchantment—God or the Devil. Inside the United Nations, delegations and Secretariat officials, naturally resenting the diabolic diagnosis, lean towards a collective identification with God. They know—at least at times they are forced to know—that their action is symbolic, the action of a play. Yet they often behave as if they also know that their action reflects a higher purpose and that the drama is a sacred one.

---

[9] *Continuing Debate*, p. 19—the parenthesis after 'Russia' and the exclamation mark are Mr. Owsley's.

2

IT WILL be said that the assimilation of the United Nations to drama—sacred or not—is no more than a metaphor. It is a metaphor and yet more than a metaphor, because the United Nations itself is a structure of metaphors. It may be safer to approach this structure in terms of recognised metaphor—the relevance of which one must try to demonstrate at every stage—than in literal and legalistic terms which tend, by their ordinary associations, to shut out from our recognition the elements of fantasy, illusion and ritual which make up so large a part of the actual life and function of the organisation. The very word 'organisation' is deceptive in that it suggests a disciplined and co-ordinated effort to reach some concrete end—like producing motor-cars, paying judges and policemen, or collecting the proceeds of slot-machines—while the United Nations moves, under the stress of conflicting impulses, and in rather chaotic ways, towards ends, which are defined only in the most general terms, and about the precise definition of which the highest management is permanently divided. To discuss this unique 'organisation' in terms appropriate to more conventional political and social structures means introducing elements of unacknowledged and therefore deceptive metaphor. A recent and elaborate study by two Yale political scientists—*World Politics in the General Assembly* by H. R. Alker and B. M. Russett—seeks, with the aid of the Yale Computer Centre and the Computation Centre at M.I.T., to use 'some of the new quantitative techniques of political science to present a factual description of the political process in the General Assembly'. The result is a collection of curious, precise and opaque data, loosely related to some dubious generalities. Results of this general character are not unusual in the present stage of what Professor Noam Chomsky has called 'the desperate attempt of the social and behavioural sciences to imitate the surface features of sciences that really have significant intellectual content'.[1] But there are special additional difficulties in the way of such an attempt where the subject of study is the United Nations. Is it possible to supply 'a factual description' of a body, or spirit, whose existence is diffused so largely in the realm of fantasy? It may be, but only if the relevance of fantasy is admitted, allowed for, and subjected to a kind of scrutiny in which Computation Centres can at present give little help.

In this case—as in the case of most—though not all—U.N. studies by political scientists—the 'reality of fantasy' is ignored. Thus Alker and Russett speak repeatedly of the 'legislative power' and 'legislative effectiveness' of the General Assembly. But the General Assembly has no legislative power and no

[1] *New York Review of Books*, 23 February, 1967.

legislative effectiveness. It has, under the Charter and also in reality, no power except the 'power to recommend'—a metaphorical form of power. The Assembly is not a legislative body except in the sense that poets are the unacknowledged legislators of mankind. A General Assembly resolution has the force of law in the same sense as has a sacred song: it provides spiritual encouragement and comfort and induces a sense of collective righteousness and of the legitimacy of a common endeavour. Political scientists who use about the United Nations language properly applicable to national parliaments are speaking metaphorically without seeming to realise it; they are speaking of the General Assembly *as if* it were a real Parliament, and thereby building into their 'factual description' an aspiration for the future, disguised as a present reality. By refusing to recognise the existence of fantasy, they actually help to extend its sway. This is not just an isolated verbal infelicity; throughout this work—which I single out, because it is the most elaborate and painstaking modern 'United Nations study' by political scientists —the parliamentary metaphor is diffused, giving a misleading impression of solidity and power in the institution studied. It is admitted that there are 'differences between national systems and the international model here studied' but the differences listed do not include the basic one: that the 'national systems' have practical power and the 'international model' has only the kind of power that we associate with poetry and religion. A national parliament is an actual money bank, in the sense of Butler's *Erewhon*: the General Assembly is a 'musical bank', a repository for our highest aspirations, but not for the lodgement of more material power.

Yet the cynicism of a Samuel Butler is appropriate only within strict limits. It is a necessary tool, in any enquiry into the United Nations, in order to cut through the layers of hokum with which the subject is surrounded, so as to penetrate to the underlying realities, and understand, among other things, the purposes which the hokum is designed to serve. But the cynicism, necessary in the *approach* to the United Nations, must at some point be made to yield to reverence: the reverence which is appropriate to the essence of an institution which is humanity's prayer to itself to be saved from itself. The prayer is acted out through a spectacle which is often absurd and even ignominious: the spectator must remind himself that behind all the nonsense remains the dimension of the sacred. Like the liturgy according to Guardini the typical United Nations spectacle is '*zwecklos aber doch sinnvoll*'—pointless but full of meaning. It is not easy for a United Nations person to keep this always in mind, because the nearer one comes to the stage the more liable one is to become disgusted with the farce and to forget its sacred function. In particular the young and innocent, who have accepted, and perhaps helped to disseminate, the idealised version, are liable to suffer from shock when they have had the opportunity for a closer look. The following revealing passage about the guides who show visitors round the U.N. Headquarters occurs in a useful factual publication, with no pretensions to irony, the *Follett Vest-Pocket Handbook on the United Nations:*

'The guides are not part of the regular Secretariat staff but are hired under special service contracts. Qualifications are a college degree or its equivalent. The term of guide duty has a limit, which is two years and three months. It is limited because experience has shown that when a guide keeps her job any longer, she loses some of the enthusiasm she is otherwise able to communicate to the United Nations visitors.'[2]

Experience has now shown that loss of enthusiasm is not confined to the girl guides. The guide of guides, the Undersecretary for Public Information at the United Nations (and signatory of the introduction to the *Follett Vest-Pocket Handbook*) was from 1960–65 a Brazilian journalist, Hernane Tavares de Sá, who has now written an important book called *The Play Within the Play: the Inside Story of the U.N.* The image is sustained in section-headings, 'The Plot', 'The Angels' (in the theatrical, not theological, sense), 'The Players', 'The Stage', etc.—and it is interesting that this language should suggest itself to one who, within the structure so conceived, performed a function of assistant stage-manager. The text itself does not generally develop or explore the metaphor—it is no more than that to Mr de Sá—but is, as the publishers state, 'a sharp exposé, by turns serious and gossipy, informative and entertaining, of what really goes on in the glass house on the East River and in its counterpart in Geneva'. *The Play Within the Play* in fact belongs with the present writer's *To Katanga and Back* and General von Horn's *Soldiering for Peace* on the very small shelf of books by people who have experience of important phases of U.N. activity and who have chosen to exercise candour—of which the other name is indiscretion—in writing about their U.N. experience. To those who have worked for the U.N., *The Play Within the Play* will bring in the main, confirmatory detail—often amusing—of what they already know, although most of them do not tell it. The book should give pause, however, to the many outside students of the U.N., including many academic writers on the subject, who have on the whole accepted the officially propagated 'image' of the U.N. For here the chief custodian of that

[2] *Follett Vest-Pocket Handbook on the United Nations* (Chicago, 1965).

image turns iconoclast. Mr Tavares de Sá tells us that 'the public image of the U.N.'—which is 'moulded in a large degree by the news about the U.N. filtered from the senior officials of the organisation's various departments, members of delegations and the governments themselves'—'has little to do with the facts of life on the East River'. The following are examples of some of these 'facts of life':

'If Washington does not want something to be done either by the General Assembly or by the Security Council (and without having to use its veto power) it will simply not be done. . . . Any initiative of genuine scope by the U.N. must satisfy political needs and interests of American foreign policy. . . . U.N. action will never serve the interests of the URSS [sic] or of the Soviet bloc except in those occasional instances where there is a Soviet-American coincidence of interests; but U.N. action will (and often does) go counter to the interests of the Soviet bloc. . . . [The] hallowed system of neutralising all Russians inside the Secretariat has been in operation from the beginnings of the United Nations. . . . The United Nations is not an international body but rather a dependency of the United States that has been in recent years infiltrated by the Afro-Asians. . . .'[3]

The last of these statements involves—as I shall try to show—an element of distortion, resulting from a failure, or unwillingness to assess in any depth the real function of the U.N. The other statements are all true—at least they are true statements about the way in which the United Nations has worked up to now; the use of the future tense in some of them may be misleading. The academic and other writers who have sought to controvert such statements in the past have been doing so on the basis of the kind of statement that used to be cleared for issue through the office of the Undersecretary for Public Information. The information often issued otherwise than through the Office of Public Information; some writers on international politics who would not uncritically accept a 'release', so marked, will easily swallow the same information, imparted 'confidentially' in an office on the 38th floor. The dose will be the same, in its political essence, as that dispensed to the public by the Office of Public Information; only the method of administration differs. The method is important, however: certain academics have no resistance at all to confidential tidings imparted in suitable surroundings by officials of high rank and appropriate demeanour. But since all the information was by definition what the Secretariat wanted to divulge, all of it that was important (apart from personal gossip, which has of course a kind of importance) also went out

[3] *The Play Within the Play: the Inside Story of the U.N.* (New York, 1966).

through the Office of Public Information, to the press and public at large. The authority of the former controller of the office can now be invoked against the accuracy of the information. The former Undersecretary 'suspected', in the introduction to his book, that there is no contemporary political institution 'where appearances so belie realities'. From the man who bore the primary responsibility for the 'appearances' during five critical years of the organisation's life, this is a remarkable admission.

3

ALTHOUGH *The Play Within the Play* does not make use of the image of a puppet theatre, and although its author by no means agrees with left-wing critics of the United Nations, the 'realities' which the book brings to light, from behind the 'appearances' which its author formerly projected, obviously do much to corroborate the often-heard left-wing charges that the proceedings on the East River are a puppet show of which the wires are pulled from Washington. There has always been more substance in such charges than most admirers of the United Nations like to think, and more than most academic analysts suggest. I have discussed this elsewhere—in *To Katanga and Back* (1962) and in an essay in *Writers and Politics* (1965)—reaching substantially the same conclusions, on the subject of Washington's influence, as have now been formulated by the ex-Undersecretary. The facts are well known to everyone who has worked at the United Nations—or at any rate to everyone who has worked there for at least that fateful period of two years and three months, at the end of which the girl guides are held to have lost their political innocence, otherwise known as their 'enthusiasm'. It is sufficient to cast a reasonably attentive look at the working of any of the three principal organs of the United Nations to be satisfied of the pervasive and predominant influence which the United States has exercised in the organisation. One also becomes aware, however, that the influence is exercised in conditions of increasing delicacy and that the puppet image—though more suggestive and less outrageous than Western spokesmen claim—is not really adequate or appropriate. The drama is of another, and more exciting kind.

The General Assembly, the main theatre of the United Nations, is the best place in which to begin a consideration of the dramatic interplay in which the United States and the United Nations are involved. The Assembly is sometimes dismissed as having 'no real power'; in fact none of the organs has any real, in the sense of material, power; the Assembly is the main focus of such power as does reside in the United Nations—moral, imaginative, religious power. Not that the Assembly is, in itself, especially moral, imaginative or religious, but that the corresponding human qualities act on and through it, in surprising and unpredictable ways.

In the Assembly any delegate soon learns that the most important thing to know in relation to any proposition is how the United States stands on it. Where the United States has been flatly opposed, the proposition has had no chance of being carried. Where the United States has been indifferent—a rare event—the proposition, even if carried, has had no practical significance. There has been all the difference in the world between an

Assembly resolution, *actively supported by the United States*, and a resolution passed by a similar numerical majority but with the United States abstaining, or even casting a merely tactical vote in favour. In the former case the resolution has constituted a 'moral warrant' for a policy which the most powerful country in the world either intends to execute or finds it otherwise useful to have proclaimed; resolutions not actively supported by the United States have remained unheeded 'recommendations', like the long series of Assembly resolutions on *apartheid*. It is true—and potentially important—that this need not always remain so. In certain conditions, another great power could conceivably avail itself of the Assembly's 'moral warrant'. Britain and France have not the influence to gather an Assembly majority for a policy of their own choosing—as was demonstrated with overwhelming conclusiveness at the time of Suez—and would be actively opposed to the implementation of any policy likely to emerge from a 'spontaneous' majority of the poor and coloured nations. As regards influence, the Soviet Union is in a similar position; the Soviet Delegation cannot muster more than ten safe votes for a policy of its own choosing. But it is not inconceivable that the Soviet Union might, in certain circumstances, volunteer its services for the execution of the substance of an Assembly resolution, whose sponsors were numerous but too weak to execute it themselves. The 'moral warrant' theory, recognising a reserve of sacred authority in the Assembly, has explosive potentialities, like everything sacred.

The State Department has no doubt perceived that the problem of South-West Africa has ominous possibilities in the direction of a sacred overflow. That is to say, this is one case in which the Soviet Union may some day have the opportunity and perhaps the motive, to emulate certain past performances of the United States, by emerging in the character of Champion of the United Nations, invested by the Assembly in solemn ceremonial with the moral authority to undertake a legitimate feat of arms.

It is relevant to consider, in a little detail, how such a major diversion in the flow of United Nations charisma might be brought about. The following is intended, not as a prediction, but as the construction of a model to illustrate the potentialities of the legitimising function of the United Nations.

The General Assembly has already 'decided', in the Session of 1966, that South Africa's right to be in South-West Africa derived solely from the Mandate conferred on it by the League of Nations, that that mandate has been terminated, and that the United Nations must take over the administration of South-West Africa. The General Assembly's competence to do all this might be challenged by international lawyers, especially those retained by the Republic of South Africa. From the standpoint of international politics, however, what is important is not what lawyers may think, or say, but the fact that both the United States and the Soviet Union, by voting in favour, have committed themselves to the position that the Assembly's 'decision' is valid. That is to say the Assembly is felt to have performed a rite in virtue of which a certain political situation becomes unholy. It is really a sort of solemn curse. The question then arises as to what, if anything, either or both of these Powers will do to make the 'decision', or curse, effective.

For the United States, Ambassador Goldberg, in the Assembly, stressed the desirability of 'concrete', 'effective' and 'practical' measures to implement the decision. What these measures should be is a question that was referred to a Commission. The Soviet representative on the Commission has pointed out that such measures are likely to require military action, and he is probably right: the late Hendrik Verwoerd is reported to have said that 'if the United Nations want South-West Africa they can come and get it'. Britain, and probably France, would be opposed to such action; the United States, it must be assumed, does not desire it, but obviously does not desire, either, to appear, especially in the overwhelmingly non-white Assembly, in the role of 'protector of South Africa'. As far as the Security Council is concerned, the position—from a Western or a South African point of view—is 'safe'. Even if a majority there should favour military action, Britain can certainly be counted on to vote against (thereby applying its 'veto'), unless the United States applies financial pressure so heavy as to counterbalance Britain's large financial stake in South Africa; the United States can be counted on, with almost equal certainty, not to apply such pressure in this case. Were the Security Council all that had to be taken into account, the United States could even permit itself to vote *in favour* of military action against South Africa—safe in the knowledge that, under article 27 of the Charter, such a vote would be without effect, lacking the 'concurring vote' of another permanent member—Britain—so that America could be, once more, safely and blissfully 'paralysed' as on Hungary.

The situation in the General Assembly, however, is much less reassuring from an American point of view. The 'spontaneous' tendency of African delegates, faced—as they are almost certain to be—with complete intransigence on the part of South Africa, is likely to be towards a vote in favour of military action. The United States and its allies will probably be able to head off such a development for a considerable time. The African states are poor and need aid: their delegates do not always feel as strongly as they sound on the subject of South Africa: the

United States itself can influence many African votes in varying degrees and can probably count, if necessary, on Malawi. the Congo (Leopoldville), Liberia and Ethiopia. France has a powerful influence—if she chooses to exert it—over most of her former colonies: Britain has a vaguer and more marginal influence, unlikely to be of much service on such a subject as this: South Africa itself can probably influence some African votes—when it heeds them, as certainly on this. With these advantages an African consensus in favour of military action can at least be delayed. It is not sure, however, that it can be indefinitely prevented. It is hard to eat high words in public, and African governments and delegates have used very high words about South Africa. It is also more difficult, and felt to be somehow less legitimate, to 'squeeze' a government about an issue lying in what is thought of as its own terrain—an African Government on an African subject—than it is to 'squeeze' one on a matter which is thought of as remote, and no proper business of the country concerned—an African government on Chinese representation, say. Also African governments and delegates may be taken, by an emotional shock, out of the positions assigned to them by the rational calculations of those who seek to manage voting in the Assembly.

Another 'Sharpeville', a second 'murder of Lumumba' might detonate an African consensus on a resolution in favour of military action to expel South Africa from South-West Africa. In such circumstances it might be difficult for the United States to be seen to oppose such a resolution, or to apply any strong pressure on others to oppose it. Assembly resolutions on important questions require, of course, a two-thirds majority and it is always possible for the United States to muster—from among the Latin American and other satellites (e.g. the Republic of China, Laos and Thailand)—votes—at least a blocking third—against any measure which it opposes, especially a measure on which, as in this case, vigorous and spontaneous support for the American position would be forthcoming from Western Europe. On this particular issue, however, it would be embarrassing for the United States to be seen to block, in this way, a resolution backed by an African consensus, for the only effective 'last resort' action against an illegal white occupier of African territory. It is therefore quite within the bounds of possibility that the General Assembly will, one day, recommend—it is likely to say 'decide' but the Charter only gives it power to recommend—military action against South Africa in South-West Africa. It seems to be generally assumed that such a resolution would be without effect, since the African states would be powerless to implement it, and the United States would not take the lead in implementing it. It certainly would be without effect, *unless the Soviet Union should decide to back its implementation*. If it did so, it could cite (or more probably, African participants could cite for it) the 'Uniting for Peace' resolution of 1950 (see p. 127 below)—the legality of which it contested at the time and still contests up to now—under which the General Assembly, at the instance of the United States—provided 'moral warrant' for the continuation of the United States action in Korea in 1950 (after the Soviet Union's return to its Security Council seat had deadlocked the Council). It is true that the Soviet Union has, until very recently, resisted the tendency of the Assembly to 'usurp' the role of the Security Council, and that it took this position in relation to the Assembly resolution in 1967, aimed at setting up a United Nations administration for South-West Africa. But this Soviet position cannot be regarded as permanently fixed. In the Middle Eastern crisis of 1967, it was the Soviet Union which took the initiative of having the General Assembly convened after the failure of the Security Council to agree: a significant adoption of a procedure formerly followed by the United States, and deplored by the Soviet Union. And if the General Assembly can properly be asked to pronounce on such a theme at all, is it not legitimate for a group of Powers to act on its recommendations—citing, or refraining from citing, the precedent of 'Uniting for Peace'?

This precedent—and similar ones following the Council deadlock on the Middle East (1956) and the Congo (1960)—would make it extremely difficult for the United States to contest the legitimacy of a decision by a group of nations to act on an Assembly recommendation—the more so as it would be a decision to expel a country from a territory in which, according to the recorded, official position of the United States, that country has no right at all to be. If the Soviet Union decided to equip, and participate in, a military action, recommended by the General Assembly—and thus sanctioned by a ritual recognised as holy by the United States—for the expulsion of South African forces from the territory of South-West Africa, of which these forces are acknowledged to be in illegal occupation, could the United States effectively discourage, or resist, such action? It seems doubtful: the United States might, in the last resort, deem it the lesser evil to participate in the action itself.

It is true that a Soviet decision to intervene hardly seems consonant with the cautious politics which the Soviet Union has pursued since the fall of Khrushchev. It cannot, however, safely be assumed that such caution will always continue. If the military advisers of the Soviet Government report that the resources available are such as to guarantee the success of such an expedition—granted that the United States does not come in on the other side—that Government might conceivably decide that the advantages to be derived from it outweighed its cost. The humiliations of the Congo and Cuba would be wiped out; the prestige of the liberator of Southern Africa—for such a war would be likely to involve no less—might well outshine, throughout the coloured world, that of the United States and of China. In any case the mere fact that such an option may become open has a weight of its own. The otherwise surprisingly 'forward' position which the United States delegation has taken up on this matter, may have its origin in the desire not to allow the Soviet Union to assume the leadership, as far as the great Powers are concerned, on this issue. If so, this is a competition which may be heavy with consequences for the rulers of Southern Africa.

I should add that I have discussed this line of possibility (Soviet action under 'Uniting for Peace' in relation to South-West Africa) with two senior United Nations delegates, one British and one African, and both indicated their disbelief in it. The British delegate thought it inconceivable that the Russians would ever go to such lengths on an African issue. The African delegate insisted that the question of action was strictly one for the Security Council, and not within the competence of the Assembly; it was the duty of the Security Council to act. From the two reactions I took it that a 'Uniting for Peace' action on South-West Africa was not on anyone's agenda for the near future. The existence of the possibility, however, remains for the longer term and affects choices in the shorter; I thought that both my interlocutors looked a little worried at the mere mention of the subject. It is of course also theoretically conceivable that the Soviet Union could intervene in the Middle East to implement an Assembly resolution. But this is more improbable than such a move in relation to South-West Africa, and this for two connected reasons. First, the Assembly is unlikely ever to pass the kind of resolution that could constitute clear 'moral warrant' for Soviet intervention. The United States would vigorously and openly oppose such a resolution, and resolutions so opposed do not pass—witness the decisive rejection of the Soviet and Albanian 'anti-Israel' resolutions by the General Assembly in July, 1967. Second, the Soviet Union knows that the United States is committed to Israel in a way in which it is not committed to South Africa, and that a Soviet attack on Israel would be likely to lead to general war. On the other hand, it would be very difficult for the United States to take up arms in order to defend South Africa's right to remain in a place where the United States has publicly affirmed that South Africa has no right to be.

Discussion of the potentialities of the South-West Africa question illustrates rather well the present dimensions and limitations of United States influence in the Assembly and also—and this is what invalidates the 'puppet' theory—the kind of influence which the General Assembly may exert over the great powers, including the United States. For the United States is to some extent the prisoner of the image of the United Nations, and in particular the General Assembly, which it has itself created. In the years from 1945 to 1958—when the United States had a safe two-thirds majority in the Assembly—United States spokesmen sought to establish the theory that the Assembly was, in Warren Austin's words, 'the moral conscience of the world'. Why the delegates of the Saudi Arabian, Royal Laotian, South African, Dominican Republican, Haitian, British, Irish and other governments should, when met together to vote, form such an entity as a collective 'moral conscience' was never explained, and all that the doctrine really meant at that time was that if the United States required legitimation of any given course of action, it could at that time be sure of getting it from the General Assembly by a safe two-thirds majority.

At the time when the two-thirds majority began to look less safe, it became necessary to take an apprehensive look at the moral authority of the Assembly. Thus at the very end of the period when the United States still enjoyed its safe majority Mr Ernest W. Lefever, in a timely study commissioned by the Church Peace Union, wrote as follows:

> Until recent years, the moral status of majority decisions at the United Nations was not a live issue in the free world, since [sic] the West always had the assurance of sufficient votes in the Assembly to uphold its policy on any important issue. But with the admission of many new members from Africa and Asia, the West can no longer depend on a working majority to support its position....
>
> An American policy of relying on and complying with the majority decisions of the United Nations is tenable only as long as the United States believes these decisions to be just and right from her point of view. With the present composition and voting patterns of the General Assembly, the time may not be far distant when the United States can no longer accept the moral validity of a majority vote.[1]

In 1958—the year following the publication of Mr Lefever's ethico-political ruminations—the General Assembly failed to provide the required endorsement for the Anglo-American interventions in Lebanon and Jordan. The pro-West 'working majority', which provided the basis for the 'moral status' of majority decisions, in the eyes of the West had unmistakably

---

[1] *Ethics and United States Foreign Policy*, 1957, p. 95.

crumbled. Such decisions have not yet however lost *all* their 'moral validity', since the United States has power to influence them and to block anything to which it is definitely opposed. The absolutely safe two-thirds majority has gone, but the aura of moral validity with which the United States long invested such majorities lingers on—despite Mr Lefever and others—among the American public and to a lesser extent elsewhere. Uncle Sam is caught in his own scenario, somewhat to his present embarrassment, and possibly to his greater future embarrassment.

The present is a delicate transitional phase. United States spokesmen wish to reduce the intensity of that halo—in case the 'moral conscience' should one day turn and bite them—but they don't wish to reduce it too much; after all the United States still has far greater influence in the General Assembly than any other power, and the Assembly's utility to United States policy is by no means exhausted. Thus the possible future use of the Assembly combines with the uses made of it in the past to make its present management a matter of considerable importance and delicacy for the United States. Professor Inis L. Claude, of Michigan, probably the most penetrating American analyst of the United Nations, recognised this in a 1961 contribution to a symposium: 'Our occasional insistence that it is both desirable and possible for the United Nations to function as an impartial agent, serving the real interests of both sides by filling a vacuum neutrally and thereby reducing the tendency of Cold War blocs to move into it competitively, has been confused and made less credible by our more general tendency to regard the organisation as an instrument to be used by the West in the struggle against the East. The ambiguity eats deep into our own thinking; we should like the organisation to be able to alternate between serving Western interests and presiding with what everyone must regard as majestic impartiality over the interests of the contending blocs . . . Our recent anxieties about the organisation stem largely from the recognition that the era of Western dominance in its political processes is passing or has passed.'[2] Elsewhere in the same essay Professor Claude recognises the routine dramatic function of the United Nations: 'It can be used to dramatise the common interest in seeking such diminution of tensions as may be essential to the avoidance of general war.'[3] It can—and the fact is of great importance—but it can also be used to dramatise other things, such as the legitimation of an anti-Soviet move by the United States.

The process whereby involvement in the ritual drama produces unpredictable commitments was discerned and in part

[2] *The United States and the United Nations*, pp. 122-3.
[3] Ibid, p. 113.

deprecated by Dag Hammarskjold, in an address at Berkeley in 1955. Speaking of what he called 'conference diplomacy' he said: 'It can activate the sound instincts of the common man in favour of righteous causes. It can educate and guide. But it has, also, weaknesses. There is the temptation to play to the gallery at the expense of solid construction. And there is the risk that positions once taken publicly become frozen, making compromise more difficult.'[4] Paradoxically, however, it seems to be mainly through this process of 'freezing' that change occurs at, and through, the United Nations. There can be little doubt that when Mr Goldberg made his remarkable statement on South-West Africa he was playing to an African gallery at the Assembly. By this ploy, the United States has publicly committed itself to 'practical', 'effective' and 'concrete' measures to bring about changes which another country has indicated its determination to resist, by force if necessary. There may well be those—in the State Department, the Pentagon and Western Europe—who will feel that the dangers of playing to the gallery are not simply those of immobility and rigidity as Hammarskjold seems to suggest: this is a case where the 'freezing' involves—from their point of view—the danger of skidding into a collision course. But from the point of view of the Africans, the case is a satisfactory demonstration of the moral pressure which they can exert, through the theatre of the Assembly, on a great power and, through that power, on the last sovereign stronghold of open contempt.

[4] *Dag Hammarskjold, Servant of Peace*, p. 95.

4

IN THE subways and other public places in New York, a coloured poster invites: 'COME TO THE U.N.: A trip to the United Nations Headquarters can be educational and inspirational. What's more it's fun.' Three delegates are in the picture. One is a pretty Japanese girl in national dress; the second a smiling Mr Goldberg. The third, a large figure in the middle, has his back to the camera. From his robes and from the visible portion of the back of his neck and left jaw, it is permissible to infer that he is an African. It is also permissible to infer that those responsible—presumably Mr Tavares de Sá's Office of Public Information—for the advertisement had their reasons for placing him with his back to the camera.

In any case, the picture is not without symbolic value. In the Assembly also, since 1960, the African bulks large, is in the centre of the stage and is a source of embarrassment and alarm. He bulks large because African delegations now constitute about one-third of the Assembly. He is in the centre of the stage, because the continent of Africa, with the Middle East, constitute the 'open' area in respect of which the Powers compete, or try to reach consensus, at and through the United Nations. (Europe, East and West, is too powerful to be much affected, in its domestic concerns, by what happens at Turtle Bay; the Western Hemisphere is normally an American 'closed shop'; the pretence that Formosa is China effectively keeps the United Nations from playing at present any significant role in the Far East.) The African is a source of embarrassment because of the racially-aligned power structure both in the United Nations itself and in the host country. At the United Nations, four of the five permanent Members of the Security Council are white, and the representation of the only coloured country (China), which is a Permanent Member, has been determined by the most powerful white country, the United States, by the use of financial and diplomatic pressures applied to poor and weak states, most of which have coloured populations. The Asian Uncle Tom on the Security Council, and the need to acquiesce in his maintenance there, are standing symbols, in this symbolic world, of the continued subjection of the non-white majority of the human race. African delegates have only to take a walk in Manhattan to meet other, more tangible and personal, reminders of the same thing. These delegates are likely to bring back into the debates of the Assembly some of the tensions and resentments generated by the hostile environment.

From experience Mr Tavares de Sá writes about the African diplomats: 'They were drinking in large gulps the glamour and glitter of New York, but choking on rebuffs and humiliations in the city's hotels and restaurants—some only imagined but others only too real.' Whites, and especially Americans, find this resentment difficult to cope with, and themselves become unstable and unpredictable in their reactions. Among liberals, a more or less clear conviction that 'racism is wrong' often has a troubled co-existence with more or less deep-seated feelings of hostility and fear. Such feelings can produce a certain political inconsequence. Thus Mr Goldberg, clearly a liberal, complained to a gathering of American Negroes about the 'irresponsibility' of African delegates, to please whom he had just made far-reaching pledges on behalf of his country. Among non-liberals—a much more numerous class at the United Nations than one would gather from public pronouncements—bitter contempt for Africans has to be masked, while actually working at or for the United Nations, but can emerge afterwards. Thus General van Horn, who from 1958 to 1963, held important 'peace-keeping' commands for the United Nations in the Middle East and Africa, writes in the following vein about a visit to U.N. Headquarters:

'... They [new states] were using their inflated importance to band together to become a pressure group which was slowly but surely transforming the United Nations into a forum for racial hatred.... Everywhere there were eager little groups of Africans in animated discussion whose [sic] rather conspiratorial look would suddenly evaporate when a white girl joined their small, enclosed ring. I saw this happen on so many occasions—the lone white girl surrounded by a circle of beaming black faces—that I was hard put not to recall the rumours about enterprising states enlisting appreciative sympathy amongst these delegates by politically-sponsored call-girl operations.... It was plain that for some nations who wanted to make friends and influence people, white girls were a useful adjunct to financial and technological aid to underdeveloped countries. Altogether it was a gloomy homecoming.'[1]

Mr Tavares de Sá shares the General's basic attitudes and has his own version of the ethno-politico-erotic reverie: 'These were the years when fair British royalty would be photographed dancing with jet-black African potentates and their wives.'[2]

The Swedish Force Commander and the Brazilian Undersecretary are, I think representative of much 'white' opinion at the U.N. and their reminiscences reveal the suppressed part of the 'white' reaction to the large increase in African membership from 1960 on. Suppressed, because of course on the outside all was cordiality; officially all delegations welcomed the African

[1] *Soldiering for Peace*, London, 1966, p. 288.
[2] *The Play Within the Play*, p. 123.

'... the choice of Nuremberg for the scene of the trials (though probably fortuitous) seemed to symbolise the idea that a special new "sacred drama" was required to exercise the power of the old one, and must be enacted in the same place ... The reprobates, "like stinking goats", were seen being lowered to damnation. As theatre, it was very simple and very effective; as ritual it derived power from ancient belief, and from humanity's apparently ineradicable wish to punish and to be absolved. Guilt was buried with the captives.' (pages 281–2)

1946
-1961

Flushing Meadows, Long Island, U.S.

U.N.O. on HUNGARY and SUEZ

Page from Topolski's Chronicle 1956

TOPOLSKI's CHRONICLE

...nothing affirmeth and therefore never lyeth. — Sir Philip Sidney (1580)

Established 1953

Nos. 16-21 (196-201) Vol. IX 1961

STOP PRESS
WAR IN SPACE?

Professor Sir Bernard Lovell, F.R.S. of the Jodrell Bank Experimental Station said of the American Satellite, carrying 350 million copper needles into space: "The project does not represent a scientific experiment, but has been devised by U.S. military scientists..."

UNITED NATIONS
MULTIPLIES AND SO FOUNDERS

The reigning fallacy—*not man but nation as humanity's unit*—ceases to be convenient. U.S. NEWS & WORLD REPORT says: "... Until recently the U.S. and its allies could easily muster the votes to control the U.N. ASSEMBLY. This is no longer true..."

Page from Topolski's Chronicle 1961

influx, and all members of the Secretariat were by definition free from racial as from national prejudice. No Undersecretary —least of all one in charge of Public Information—and no Force Commander—least of all the Commander in the Congo— could afford, while in office, to give any sign of 'hate-black'. Yet smouldering underneath was the fear of black magic; the Caucasian mind set up its own interior *Ballet Africain*, in which a Communist Mephistopheles prostitutes white womanhood to Negro lust, and the Negro goes on to the ceremonial defilement of European sacred personages.

What relevance does this intimate drama, within the Caucasian *camera obscura*, behind the correct facade of the international civil servant and the neutral soldier, have to the external political drama on the stage of the Assembly? According to Mr Tavares de Sá—who reveals rather than acknowledges the existence of this particular play within the play—it could have no continuing relevance, because African influence is itself played out. The great African scenes of 1960 were a flash in the pan: the 'wind of change' that Mr Macmillan felt in that year has died away.

'The situation has changed beyond recognition', according to *The Play Within the Play*, 'in the five years from 1960 to 1965. For all their [sic] rantings in the General Assembly, and the collective bad manners such as walking out on Prime Minister Harold Wilson when he addressed a plenary session in the autumn of 1965, African influence as such has virtually ceased to exist. Only within the large Afro-Asian bloc and then by negotiating beforehand with the U.S. delegation, can the Africans make their will felt on anything but the most innocuous U.N. activities.'[3]

The explanation which the former Undersecretary offers for this 'swift African eclipse' is that 'mesmerised by the high jinks in the Assembly where everyone appeared to take them seriously', the Africans neglected 'the U.N.'s vital centre of power'[4] by failing to secure significant positions within the Secretariat.

Now Mr Tavares de Sá is an experienced and fairly shrewd observer, but his perspective here is doubly distorted. It is distorted first by his obvious dislike of Africans, engaged before his mind's eye in an eternal slow waltz with Princess Margaret, and by his desire to cut them down to size. The second cause of distortion is the opinion, endemic in the Secretariat, that it is in the Secretariat that the U.N.'s power lies. It is extraordinary how often U.N. people—who know very well that the U.N. does not

---

[3] *The Play Within the Play*, pp. 123-4.
[4] Ibid, p. 124.

have any real power, in the sense in which the real world uses the term—solemnly discuss the question of where, in which organ, the 'real power' lies. (Mr de Sá actually situates the power exclusively in two different places: The 'vital centre of power' is in the Secretariat, p. 124, and 'the only real power the U.N. possesses is in the [Security] Council, p. 53.) The fact is that, the U.N. being—as Christopher Caudwell said about religion generally—'a reality, but a *fantastic* reality', its power is also primarily fantastic. And the main seat of the fantastic power is the main theatre: the General Assembly.

The Secretariat has always had difficulty in acknowledging this prime fact. Hammarskjold, like Trygve Lie before him, liked to lay public stress on the importance of 'quiet diplomacy', and to suggest that what went on 'behind the scenes' was more important than what went on on the brightly-lit stage of the Assembly and the Councils. This theory has been adopted by the Secretariat generally. Yet there would be no 'behind the scenes' were it not for 'the scenes' themselves. Arrangements that are worked out behind the scenes—as all practical arrangements must be—have to be of such a nature that they can then be acted out, hopefully to the satisfaction of those who arranged them, on the stage of the Assembly or the Security Council. The stage is therefore always in the minds of those who are behind the scenes: it dominates their action, as it is intended to dominate the imagination of those who will watch the spectacle. This situation can be frustrating for those members of an essentially dramatic organisation who never appear on stage, or have only an occasional walk-on part. This does not apply to the Secretary-General, always a significant and sometimes an exceedingly impressive figure on the stage itself, and having the right, under article 99 of the Charter, to write and speak his own lines. The great mass of Secretariat officials have obviously no such opportunity, and even the highest, below the Secretary-General, are usually unknown to the general public and often (with a few exceptions including the Secretaries to the main Committees) little known and little esteemed by Delegates generally. This is not like the anonymity of the Civil Servant, within a national service; the British Civil Servant can take pride in the fact that he gets on with the job, while his Minister does the talking. But in the United Nations it is 'the talking', the affecting of international public opinion, which is of prime importance, while the job performed by the international civil servant is often trivial or meaningless. Mr Tavares de Sá acknowledges that 'several hundred Secretariat staff members from the lowly P.1.'s to the semi-exalted P.5's, D1's and D2's have nothing to do'[5] (readers

[5] *The Play Within the Play*, p. 157.

will miss some of the flavour of this if they do not know that the highest of the 'semi-exalted' ranks named comes just below that of Undersecretary) and that 'the bulk of the papers circulated in the building through the messenger service lacked any intrinsic significance'.[6]

It is true that in certain conditions—which I shall discuss later—certain U.N. officials can find themselves wielding real power, usually briefly and marginally—though sometimes momentously enough—but the Secretariat generally is mostly occupied, not with exercising power, but with performing the part of an 'international civil service': acting, in short, as if there were some kind of world government which it was serving, and thereby satisfying in fantasy a wide-spread human aspiration[7]. The individual part, within the collective one, is usually dim and unsatisfactory. The 'international civil servant' does not normally resemble very closely the national kind (or the national kind in advanced countries); he is likely to be more flamboyant and more romantic and consequently dissatisfied with the anonymous role allotted to him. A political scientist[8] has written of 'behind the scenes actors' in international politics, and the phrase has a more exact meaning than perhaps he intended: writers on international politics often seem to be obeying instructions to bring their metaphors in dead or alive. Where they exist, 'behind the scenes actors' must be frustrated hams, and many international civil servants are just that. It is natural therefore that some of them should tend to compensate by depreciating the importance of the stage, the General Assembly.

In taking possession of this stage, to the comparative neglect of the Secretariat and its supposed 'vital power', the African delegations showed a correct feeling for the nature of the United Nations and for what they could accomplish in it.

Mr Tavares de Sá contrasts the supposed folly of the Africans, beguiled by the bright lights of the Assembly, with the astute conduct of the Indians who secured 'an entire chain of command' in the Secretariat. But there is no evidence that the 'Indian chain of command' ever served any significant Asian, Indian or other avowable purpose; the very phrase 'chain of command' is illusory in an organisation whose only power is symbolic and diffuse. In the days when Indians were really influential in U.N. international politics—as distinct from the office politics of the Secretariat—their weight was felt in the Assembly and the

---

[6] *The Play Within the Play*, p. 154.

[7] I am here referring, as elsewhere in this book, to the working of the U.N. (including the Secretariat) as a *political* institution. These remarks are therefore not intended to apply to technical personnel, etc.

[8] Arnold Wolfers 'The Actors in International Politics' in *Theoretical Aspects of International Relations*, edited by W. T. R. Fox, Notre Dame, 1959.

Council. In those days Krishna Menon—whom some called the Hamlet of the U.N., and who might more appropriately have been called its Jack Cade—held the centre of the stage, and his effects were ably managed for him by India's Permanent Representative, Arthur Lall. In 1960 however, when so many Africans were added to the cast, Indians began to lose the big parts.

The Africans, perhaps because their own politics contain such large elements of symbolism and drama, seem to have grasped from the beginning the true possibilities of the United Nations. Mr Tavares de Sá's contention—in his chapter 'African Myth on First Avenue'—that 'African influence as such has ceased to exist', has not been borne out by events. U.N. proceedings in the session of 1966 were dominated by African problems—Rhodesia before the Security Council and South-West Africa before the General Assembly. Britain found itself proposing mandatory sanctions against Rhodesia, and the Security Council not merely approved but stiffened these measures—adding oil to the commodities listed, and specifically naming the Rhodesian situation as 'a threat to the peace'; a logical preliminary to sanctions, in terms of the relevant Chapter (VII) of the Charter, but a step in logic which the British Government would have preferred to pass over in silence. On South-West Africa, the United States found itself supporting the Assembly 'decision' terminating South Africa's mandate—and thereby recognised the validity of this decision; the inverted commas round this word are removed on noting American recognition. This recognition was a potentially momentous step, especially when combined with demands, by the United States, for the finding of 'concrete, effective and practical measures' to give effect to the Assembly decision.

It is safe to say that these Western powers would not have gone so far in an 'African' direction had it not been for African indignation and impatience acted out in the Assembly. There are those in the foreign offices of great powers, especially Western powers, who wonder 'what gets into' delegates to the United Nations who press their governments for authority to support propositions of this character. On conservative Western assumptions, one can fully understand this perplexity. For these simultaneous decisions have the effect of exerting significant converging pressures on the position of the Republic of South Africa, and it is known that Britain strongly wishes to avoid the building up of such pressures, while the United States at the very least has serious doubts and grave reservations about doing anything which would weaken South Africa's position. For Britain, South Africa is an important trading partner; for the

United States an ally in 'anti-communism', strategically in a key position. Yet they find themselves applying a kind of pressure to their partner and potential ally. On the South-West Africa question the pressure is direct; on the Rhodesia one, contingent. 'Not only must we proceed step by step in dealing with this situation,' said Mr George Brown on 8 December, 1966, introducing Britain's request for mandatory sanctions against Rhodesia, 'but it must not be allowed to develop into a confrontation—economic or military—involving the whole of southern Africa.' The trouble is that it is precisely 'step by step' that such confrontations are prepared. If the mandatory sanctions against Rhodesia do not work, or work too slowly, South Africa is likely to be held to have impeded and evaded them, thereby violating her Charter pledges, so that the case for sanctions against South Africa becomes much stronger. If South Africa remains simultaneously contumacious on South-West Africa, the task of those who at the United Nations, and particularly in the General Assembly, will seek to prevent sanctions against South Africa may become, in time, impossible. And as I have tried to show, in connection with South-West Africa, the 'British veto' in the Security Council is not a fully reliable shield for South Africa.

Some 'friends of South Africa' comfort themselves with the thought that the pressures which are unmistakably developing are of no consequence, being merely rhetorical and legalistic. The power of the South African army and police is real: that of the United Nations symbolic only. This is a common-sense view, but a short-sighted one; it is natural and consistent that 'the friends of South Africa' should underestimate the role of the imagination in politics and over-estimate that of the police. Rhetoric has its own dynamics, and the dynamics of a rhetoric which involves arguments of international law—when such arguments are used by those who have means to impose their concepts of international law—are powerful and dangerous. The 'power of the United Nations', and in particular of the General Assembly, is the power to evoke such rhetoric and squeeze it towards action. The legal rhetoric of a great power is a commitment, though a loose one, and this is especially so of a great power in which a government, not in control of the press and other media, has continually to persuade its own public opinion that it is doing the right thing. Once certain words have been spoken, the justifications, which must accompany future action or inaction, have been partly predetermined. And if the justifications are partly predetermined so also are the limits of action. Governments, it is true, act as a general rule not under any direct dictate of morality, but in accordance with their conception of the national interest, and of the interest of their party, and themselves. Yet no one is so cold-blooded as to be able to act like that *all* the time; sentiments, including moral sentiments, force their way in. Thus Tory policy in Central Africa in 1961, for example, was determined not solely by the balance-sheet of Tanganyika Concessions, but also by the novels of John Buchan and Rider Haggard, by nostalgia for past glory and by a certain concept of loyalty: anyone who doubts this need only read Lord Alport's reminiscences.

5

IN ORDER to understand how the powerless United Nations has none the less a certain power, especially in relation to African problems, it is necessary to say something—on the basis of observation, experience and speculation, unabetted by the Yale Computer Centre—about how morality affects politics.

He who takes the moral professions of politicians at their face value is a dolt; he who believes that morality has no effect on politics is a cynical dolt. The politician is affected, intermittently and shame-facedly, by his own personal morality; he is affected, more continuously, by what his friends will think of him, which in turn will be affected, though not uniquely shaped, by their concept of morality; finally, the politician is affected, practically and professionally, by the opinion of whatever wider public is relevant in the political system within which he works; and that opinion also will be shaped, and powerfully in relation to him, by moral concepts. These moral pressures produce a good deal of hypocrisy; they may also produce less predictable reactions:

> *It is even seen, time's something server,*
> *In mankind's medley a duty-swerver*
> *At downright 'No' or 'Yes?'*
> *Doffs all, drives straight for righteousness.*

Not often seen; but seen.

Now in relation to the question of race—the most consistent theme of the United Nations drama—Western morality is peculiarly sensitive; not because race prejudice is absent from the society, but because it is both felt as strong and felt to be wrong, so that modern Westerns behave about race almost as incoherently as Victorians did about sex. The Judaeo-Christian ethic in its post-Enlightenment form, the dominant morality in the West and powerfully affecting the rest of the world, assumes that hostility to other human beings on grounds of their racial characteristics, and oppression or ill-treatment on these grounds, are irrational and wrong. This view is generally accepted, even by people who in fact hate, despise or fear members of other races generally, or some races in particular. Now the prevalence of this acceptance—whatever feelings it may cover—means that politicians, even if they are in fact racists, or wish to pursue a policy of collusion with racists, must employ anti-racist language in public. And the very fact of this rhetorical confinement puts limits on action and on collusion, and makes a racist or pro-racist policy furtive and vulnerable.

The rule that racism must be covert has had its exceptions, and these are of such a nature as to charge the whole subject with terror and the sense of doom, and the feeling that our survival as a species is somehow at stake here. Since the Judaeo-Christian ethic assumed its post-Enlightenment form, one thinker of genius boldly and openly challenged it. Friedrich Nietzsche called racism nonsense, and disclaimed anti-Semitism, but he also called for the transvaluation of values, the reversal of the dominant ethic, the freeing of the strong from the Christian blackmail of the weak, cruelty in the place of mercy, war in the place of peace, death for the sick and the failures. Nietzsche wrote so well, and with such piercing honesty, that most writers about him are at the same time so impressed and so frightened that they try to soften his message and ignore its consequences. It is not true to say that 'Nietzsche caused Hitler' any more than to say that Rousseau caused the French Revolution; but it would be as wrong to deny that Nietzsche had anything to do with the form and intensity of the Nazi revolution as to deny that Rousseau had anything to do with those of the French Revolution. It was certainly a debased, vulgarised and partly distorted version of Nietzsche that the Nazis adopted. But had it not been for Nietzsche, what they would have had would have been the 'philosophy' of the 'Christian anti-Semites' of Nietzsche's day; a 'philosophy', that is to say, incommoded and embarrassed by the weight of the Christian vestiges and the dominant ethic. A Nazism so founded would have been a slower, more ponderous Nazism. Nietzsche on the other hand—as his radiations went out through intellectual, semi-intellectual and sub-intellectual Germany—broke the inhibitions of Christianity, and liberated racism, as Freud liberated sex. For however much Nietzsche disdained the vocabulary of racism, it was racism that he liberated; it was racism that craved the license of the strong to be cruel to the weak; or rather, whatever it is that craved this took collective and political form in racism. Even without Nietzsche, the post-1918 world would have produced its nationalist anti-Semitic demagogues and their brutal following. There is reason, however, to doubt whether, without the Nietzschean permissions, the movement would have reached such a paroxysm—whether in fact it would have got as far as the gas-chambers. Nietzsche, according to Freud, 'had a more penetrating knowledge of himself than any other man who ever lived or was ever likely to live'. If we agree with this—as most Western intellectuals would probably do—it can only be because our own self-knowledge confirms the validity of his insights. It is a disconcerting thought. What other historic events may be latent in the self revealed by Nietzsche and confirmed by Freud?

Nietzsche thought of himself not as a German but as 'a good European'; his ideas are an important part of modern European thought and of American thought; indeed the American, according to Georges Sorel, in *Reflections on Violence, is* the

Nietzschean Superman. Nietzsche's thought, and Nazi practice, are part of the history of Western man. Some American Negroes fear that, under some future stress of history, their people may meet the fate of European Jewry.

Western man [white] on his side feels the strength of his own racism: he knows he has the power. His hatred, his fear, his lust, his ethic, his power are moved by the black actors on the stage of the United Nations, and move in turn white actors there whose playing turns back again into action, unpredictably.

The gallery that the African and other actors must play to is mainly an American one. Whatever personal inconveniences the New York site of U.N. entails for Africans, it is profoundly advantageous for their dramatic impact, and therefore for their political leverage. Their audience is white America, with power in the world and Harlem on its mind. Like Hamlet's it is an audience accustomed to command, and an African could quote with perfect propriety, *The play's the thing Wherein I'll catch the conscience of the King.* Those who take the view that symbolism in politics is never of primary importance, even in such an institution as the United Nations, like to use a prosaic term of comparison: not a stage but a market. The United States, on this view, is not to be compared with a guilt-ridden hero in a drama of conscience, but with a hard-headed Yankee 'bargaining' for votes. Making the metaphor mundane, however, does not suffice to take the transaction out of the sphere of moral symbolism. A vote in the General Assembly has no significance except as a moral token: the resolutions carried by such votes, are 'recommendations' only, not binding on anyone. Why should a hard-headed bargainer enter into commitments, which may involve real action, and make concessions, which are often material, in order to acquire in return a set of moral tokens? The 'market metaphor' completely breaks down at this point, unless we are to imagine a kind of market in which a man bewitched exchanges real possessions for fairy gold—in short, if this is a market, it is a market *in a play*. The real reason why the United States needs the symbolic apparel implied in a vote, is that it wants to cut a good figure on 'the world stage' (and especially to play on the domestic stage the part of one who is cutting a good figure on the world stage).

Specifically it has valued the annual ceremony whereby the representatives of the nations act out, with their votes, the myth that they love America and hate Red China. This ceremony has been expensive to stage, probably increasingly expensive, and among its costs is the acquiring of an extra degree of sensitivity, both to voting on other issues—since the vote for keeping Formosa in China's seat can only have the required moral significance if voting generally is morally significant—and also to Afro-Asian opinion, since Afro-Asians are a majority of voters. Their votes have also an additional special significance. The presence, numbers and appearance of the delegates from Africa and Asia—especially those from Africa—are a standing reminder to the white man that he is in a minority in a world whose other inhabitants have not been given much cause to love him. White Americans are especially sensitive here, for American Negroes like to remind them that, if whites are in a majority in America, coloured people are a majority in the world. If the coloured world generally should come to feel about America as Harlem and Watts already feel about it, it is felt that something vague but terrible would happen. It becomes important then, for white Americans, both for their own re-assurance, and for the appeasement of their own Negroes, especially those who have votes—in this case real votes, not token ones—that the United States and African delegates should be seen to be on good terms. To secure this, among issues on which African delegations feel strongly, and on which certain of America's European allies also feel strongly, but in a different way, is never easy. It is a situation that leads to policies couched in ambiguous terms, interpreted in conflicting and changing ways.

The workings of dramatic interaction are well illustrated by the story of the Congo, as the United Nations became involved in it. The story opens with a notable example of symbolic and transforming racial drama: the exchange between King Baudouin of the Belgians and Patrice Lumumba at the ceremonies on the Congo's attainment of independence, 30 June, 1960. This classical exposition of the colonial record, in white and in black, ran in part as follows:

King Baudouin: Mr President, gentlemen: The independence of the Congo is the consummation of the work conceived by the genius of Leopold II, undertaken by him with tenacious courage and continued with perseverance by Belgium.

During eighty years Belgium sent to your land the best of her sons [*author's interjection: the Congolese must have wondered what the ones who were left behind were like*] first to free the Congo basin from the abhorrent slave trade which was decimating its population; then to bring together the tribes which, once enemies, are now preparing to form together the greatest of the independent States of Africa; finally, to call to a happier life the various regions of the Congo, which you represent here, united in one Parliament.

In this historic moment the thoughts of all of us must turn to the pioneers of African emancipation [*meaning Leopold II and his agents*] and towards those who, after them, have made the Congo what it is today. They deserve at the same time OUR [capitalised] admiration and YOUR [capitalised] gratitude for it is they who, devoting their efforts and even their lives to a great ideal, brought you peace and enriched your moral and material patrimony. They must never be forgotten, neither by Belgium nor by the Congo.

When Leopold II undertook the great enterprise which finds today its crown, he presented himself to you not as a conqueror but as a civiliser.

It is up to you now, gentlemen, to demonstrate that we were right to have confidence in you. . . .

Lumumba: Congolese men and women, fighters for independence victorious today, I salute you in the name of the Congolese Government. . . . As for our fate over the eighty years of colonial rule, our wounds are too fresh and too painful still for us to be able to drive them from our memory. We knew exhausting labour, wrung from us for wages which did not provide us with enough to eat, or to clothe ourselves or to bring up our children decently.

We knew sneers, insults, blows which we had to endure morning, noon and night because we were Negroes. Who will forget that to a black man one said 'tu', not certainly as a friend, but because the 'vous' of courtesy was reserved for whites only.

We knew the spoliation of our lands, in the name of texts which were supposed to be legal, but which did no more than recognise the law of the strongest.

We knew that the law was never the same for white and black; for the first it was accommodating, for the others it was cruel and inhuman. . . .

From all that, my friends, we suffered deeply.

But we, whom the votes of your representatives have chosen to direct the destinies of our dear country, we who have suffered in body and heart from colonialist oppression, we tell you out loud: from now on all that is finished.[1]

Within a few days of the Baudouin-Lumumba exchange, part of the army, the old *Force Publique*, mutinied against its white officers, and committed a number of outrages: Belgian troops, in violation of the Belgo-Congolese treaty, took possession of Elisabethville; Moise Tshombe, on the day after the Belgian troops came in, declared from Elisabethville the creation of the independent State of Katanga; the Congolese Government appealed to the United Nations for 'military aid for the protection of the Congolese national territory against the present external aggression'; and the Security Council authorised 'such military assistance as may be necessary'—without however specifying what it might be necessary for. This was on 14 July, a fortnight

---

[1] *Dossiers du C.R.I.S.P.*, 1960.

after the duologue between white king and black man who was ceasing to be his subject.

Belgians accused Lumumba of having plotted the mutinies, and some Communist spokesmen accused the 'imperialists' of having provoked them, in order to provide a pretext for intervention. Neither version has the stamp of probability and neither side produced serious evidence. Lumumba, certainly, had nothing to gain by the mutiny, and much to lose. But if the Belgians had accused him not of plotting or desiring but quite simply of *causing* the mutiny, they could have made out a powerful case, at the level of myth and symbol. The independence ceremonial had been intended to symbolise the conferring of independence on respectful blacks by noble whites and up to a point it had done so. The king had recited his dynastic myth and President Kasavubu, speaking before Lumumba, had enacted the respectful black, although with that element of ambiguity often found in respectful blacks. (It was not quite clear, for example, whether the 'heroic artisans of national emancipation' to whom Kasavubu referred in his speech on this occasion, included 'the pioneers of national emancipation' whom Baudouin had in mind; the Belgian listeners no doubt assumed that they did; the Congolese no doubt did not: one can imagine Kasavubu as happy to be interpreted in the sense that gave most satisfaction to each set of his auditors.) So far the ceremony had gone according to plan—with the President addressing the King as 'Sire'—acting out the meaning: *The Congo which is independent is the Congo which accepts the word of the white man, and hears the white man with respect. The Congo which is independent must therefore be a Congo which, in essentials, continues the Belgian Congo*. Then Lumumba—who had not been intended to speak—defied the king, rejected the myth, ruined the ceremony and broke the spell. It was not so much his words that broke the spell but that such words could be used, by a black man, to one who was, in the eyes of the Congolese, the Supreme White and that the black man went unpunished.

The Belgians present seem to have felt instinctively the ominous potentiality of this appearance of an evil fairy at the christening of the Republic. They did what they could to avert the omen. They got Lumumba to make a 'compensatory' speech rendering 'solemn homage to the King of the Belgians and the noble people whom he represents for the action accomplished here over three-quarters of a century'. In this 'compensatory' speech he also volunteered the information that 'the chief of State [*but not apparently Lumumba himself*] would spend some time in meditation before the tombs of the pioneers [*the white ones this time*] and before the statue of Leopold II, first sovereign of the Congo Free State (applause)'. All that public atonement could do to restore the power of the rite was done, but without effect; the magic was gone.

The black non-commissioned officers of the Force Publique had been told by their Commander, General Janssens, that 'After Independence = Before Independence'. He had written the words on a blackboard to make sure that they remembered them. The authority of the white officers over the black N.C.O.s and soldiers was made to rest on this assumption. The ceremonies of 30 June had been carefully designed to confirm—as far as ceremonies on such an occasion could do—the essential truth of the Janssens Doctrine. But Lumumba's intervention was the proof that the Janssens Doctrine was not true. *Before* independence no black man could with impunity have talked like that to *any* Belgian, let alone the King of them all. So 'after independence' was, after all, not the same but very different from 'before independence'. And if Lumumba, who before independence had been nobody in particular, could defy the King, why should a black N.C.O. be so respectful to a white officer, who was certainly less worthy of respect than a white King?

The duologue of 30 June was thus the signal for the events that brought in the United Nations. But it did not stop there.

Throughout the period of the U.N. presence in the Congo, the Belgians sought to re-establish the relations which the profaned rites of 30 June, 1960, had been intended to solemnise. The first success was in Katanga where a respectful black, Moise Tshombe, presided over a province-state which was all that the Belgians had intended the Republic of the Congo should be, and still intended it should become. ('The Congo,' as Baron Rothschild wrote, 'must be built up again, starting from Elisabethville.') White Americans on the whole sympathised with the Belgians; the spectacle of a Congo in which blacks mistreated whites, genuinely shocked many who were accustomed to thinking of situations in which whites mistreated blacks as being on the whole, situations of law, order and even peace. Such feelings, powerful as they were, had to be disguised in action, especially in the face of Soviet accusations: the Americans, like the Belgians, needed respectful blacks, although their views as to who should be respected were not identical. As for Hammarskjold, the logic of his position pointed in the same direction. In his mind always was the Platonic United Nations, the City of God. From the real to the ideal, the path lay through the Congo. The Congo was by far the largest task yet assigned to the United Nations, as Hammarskjold conceived it; the fiction that Korea had been a United Nations action was too crude for his taste. Success in the Congo would increase the penumbra of authority which the United Nations had begun to acquire during his Secretary-Generalship. The City of God would be a step nearer.

Yet the saint and mystic on his perilous journey had also to make practical calculations, based on the realities behind the penumbra. The priest believed in his concept of the Church, although he accepted the view that certain pious frauds were necessary to console and encourage the faithful. He knew the realities which his Undersecretary has since made public: the realities of Washington's power in and over the United Nations. He knew that if his actions—however wise they might be in relation to the realities of the Congo—displeased the United States Government, the operation would not be a success. It would be a failure. It would be proclaimed to be a failure by a majority of members of the General Assembly and the proclamation would reverberate, amplified by the U.S. Government publicity machine, through the press and media of America and much of the world. And since the United Nations is a symbolic entity, an effectively sustained proclamation of failure would constitute effective failure. To retain the confidence of the United States was therefore absolutely essential. And the confidence of the United States could be retained only by working quite closely, on important matters, with the State Department and the U.S. Embassy in Leopoldville. It is true that, in conditions of tension, this could not be done without forfeiting the confidence of the Soviet Union, thereby breaking the consensus in the Security Council. This in itself would not be fatal, provided ritual legitimation or re-legitimation could then be obtained from the General Assembly. This had been done before in relation to Korea, but then the United States had been able to command an assured two-thirds majority in the Assembly. That this was no longer so, in cases where Afro-Asian opinion was aroused, had been demonstrated in 1958, after the Anglo-American landings in Lebanon and Jordan. The successful performance of the rite in the General Assembly required at least some African participation. African opposition would be damaging, though not necessarily fatal.

In faith and intent Hammarskjold served his vision of the United Nations. In practice he was obliged to work for something that was neither the purely Platonic United Nations nor the more or less real one. Nor can the something he precisely described as an Afro-American consensus. For the American element was compact and continuous, with the solidity of the economic, military and diplomatic resources of a great power behind it. The African elements were dispersed, poorly co-ordinated, ill-informed and ill-equipped and their activities intermittent, spasmodic and divided. America had material influence over them: their influence over America was only of the moral kind, exerted through their presence and comportment in the ritual drama on the East River.

Such a script—like the Belgian script for independence day—required a respectful African, and Lumumba was not such an African. Relations with him broke down within less than a month of the arrival of the forces which various nations had contributed at the request of the Security Council and the Secretary-General. 'On our side,' writes General van Horn, 'there was no use disguising the fact that from Dag downwards there was a marked distaste and distrust for Lumumba.' Mr Tavares de Sá, for his part, writes of Hammarskjold's keeping at bay 'an ungrateful Lumumba'. What Lumumba had to be grateful for to Hammarskjold is not absolutely clear, but then Baudouin had expected him to be grateful to Leopold II; in the Congo white men seem to be as avid for black gratitude as for rubber, ivory and copper. But black gratitude is curiously rare: black ingratitude is a more familiar phase. Hammarskjold of course was in quest, not of rubber, ivory and copper, but of the Holy Grail. He could, however, be ruthless when he encountered an obstacle in his path. Lumumba was such an obstacle. There is now no doubt that persons assembled in the Congo, in the name, and armed with the moral authority, of the United Nations, played a significant and crucial part in the downfall of the Prime Minister, who had called on the United Nations for help. Miss Catherine Hoskyns[2] has established that the money with which Mobutu paid the troops with whose aid he carried out the coup of 14 September, 1960, which ejected Lumumba from office, had been provided by the United Nations four days before. (The reasons for doing this are considered below, p. 224.) United Nations forces subsequently provided protection for Lumumba at his residence—that is to say provided he kept out of active politics—but were instructed to refrain from trying to protect him if he moved outside.

Accordingly, United Nations forces made no attempt to intervene when Lumumba, having left his residence, was captured by Mobutu's troops and transferred to Tshombe's Elisabethville, where he was immediately murdered.

So far, the conduct of the United Nations operation in the Congo had followed faithfully the requirements of what was then United States policy in the Congo. Mobutu's first action after the coup had been to expel the Soviet and Czechoslovak embassies. Mobutu and Tshombe were then on good terms; no real pressure was being brought to bear on Tshombe's

[2] *The Congo Since Independence*, p. 213.

Katanga. Little concession had been made to African opinion—except for the protection extended to Lumumba at his residence—and American influence over African policies had been demonstrated by a vote in the Assembly, after Lumumba's fall; thereby—as in the annual China vote—legitimising the government of America's choice.

But in and through this world of shades and screens, Lumumba's ghost was to prove far more powerful than Lumumba. The political dynamics of ritual drama appear with particular clarity in the chain of events that followed the announcement of Lumumba's death.

It was not, to begin with, ever exactly announced. 'The Secretariat,' Hammarskjold told the Security Council on 13 February, 1961, 'has this morning received information from Elisabethville of a most serious and tragic nature, the substance of which is already well known to members.' The information was the announcement by the Minister of the Interior of Katanga that Lumumba had been killed while trying to escape. Hammarskjold did not mention Lumumba, or death, or murder.

Adlai Stevenson, who spoke next, referred to Lumumba's 'reported death', and hoped that there would be no recriminations.

Valerian Zorin, for the Soviet Union, who spoke next, was the first to use the word 'murder', from which thereafter other speakers—even including Sir Patrick Dean, representing Great Britain—did not shrink.

The Security Council met again on 15 February, amid reports of protests, demonstrations and riots in many parts of Africa and elsewhere. The relevant part of the record reads as follows:

Mr Stevenson: The issue then is simply this: Shall the United Nations survive? Shall the attempt to bring about peace by the concerted power of international understanding be discarded?

(*At this point there was a sustained interruption from the public gallery. The President ordered the gallery to be cleared and suspended the meeting until this was done.*)

Mr Stevenson: May I say that I deeply deplore this outrageous and obviously organised demonstration. To the extent that Americans may be involved I apologise on behalf of my Government to the members of the Security Council.

The *New York Times* on the following day referred to 'the most violent demonstration inside United Nations Headquarters in the world organisation's history'. Most of the demonstrators had been American Negroes, belonging to a number of different organisations. More than two dozen persons were injured.

Meanwhile condemnations and protests were pouring in not only from the more 'militant' African countries but also from some of the more 'respectful', including Nigeria and Tunisia. It was clear that African, and Afro-American, emotion was more deeply stirred than by any previous event, with the single exception of Sharpeville. Sekou Touré, President of Guinea, cabled Hammarskjold on 16 February: 'This sorry drama in which you took a predominant part despite your repeated protestations, dishonours you personally in the eyes of the embittered public of Africa and the world. Now that the curtain has fallen on the first act of your criminal tragedy, it is essential that you draw the lesson of universal condemnation from this crime.'

There falls on this debate a frightful shadow: the shadow of a lynching. Everybody knew that whites, and their servants, had thought of Lumumba as an uppity nigger, and that it was because they had thought of him in that way that he had met his death. The black man who had spoken those words of pride and defiance to the white king on his country's independence day had spoken his own death sentence, which had been executed in Elisabethville, little more than six months later, by the white man's servants. The impact of such a drama evokes powerful historical memories—of anger on the black side, guilt on the white. The black man becomes more reckless, less influenced by calculation of material advantage: the stooge becomes less reliable, the semi-stooge becomes a patriot; the voting pattern shifts; the United States no longer has a safe majority; the significance of the ritual has changed. The white man, for his part —and not only because of voting patterns—becomes anxious to propitiate. He does not want others to think of him like that, he does not want to think of himself like that. He does not want, even, to say what exactly happened. Black, for the season, has power over white. Anger and guilt converge in exacting atonement, a ceremonial act of reparation. And that act itself will serve to legitimise, in the heart of Africa, new courses of action. The white magic of the earlier U.N. resolutions is succeeded by the black magic of the Security Council Resolution of 21 February, aimed at Katanga and authorising the 'use of force if necessary in the last resort'. The idea that black magic is the bad kind is of course a white convention.

It will still be the policy of the United States that will be pursued in the Congo, but it will be a new policy. It probably would have been a new policy in some degree in any case—the Kennedy administration had just come into power—but the dramatic nature of the change, from a policy of protecting Tshombe's State of Katanga, to one of squeezing it out of existence,[3] can only be accounted for by the drama amid which the old policy had to be reconsidered. The oracle at Turtle Bay has proclaimed that Lumumba must be avenged, and paradoxically the fact that he is safely dead makes it safe to avenge him. The men in power in Leopoldville after Lumumba's fall are as respectful as Tshombe and better informed than Tshombe as to the real seat of power and focus of respect.

'It is not the Soviet Union or indeed any other big Powers who need the United Nations for their protection,' said Hammarskjold in a statement to the Assembly on 3 October, 1960, 'it is all the others. In this sense the Organisation is first of all *their* organisation . . .' At first sight this statement seems at odds with the course of the United Nations operation as I have described it. Yet it is not really so. The fact that a great power can impose its will on the ordering of the affairs of a weak country was not invented by the United Nations. What is new in the United Nations is the possibility it gives to weak nations, and black ones in particular, to act on the imagination and conscience of a great country, in the impressive setting of the Assembly Hall and the Council Chambers. This is not a wholly reliable safeguard but it is better than none at all. And Hammarskjold did not tell the weaker countries that the United Nations was '*their* organisation' absolutely; he knew very well that one power, by no means weak, exercised more authority in it than all the weak nations put together. What he told them—and he was careful about his wording—was that it was theirs 'in this sense'—the sense that they need it for their own protection. They do, and it will to some extent serve them, as long as the United States continues to feel that it needs reassurance and validation and legitimacy for its international role, and to seek these in the sacred halls of the United Nations. When the rich seek the blessing of the poor they must pay a price.

---

[3] A detailed first-hand account of the working out of the United States decision to back the use of military force by the United Nations to end the secession of Katanga is given by Roger Hilsman in Chapter 19 ('Military Force . . . and Success') of his book *To Move a Nation: the Politics of Foreign Policy in the Administration of John F. Kennedy* (New York 1967). The Secretariat still officially maintains the myth that force was not used for this purpose.

6 THE INTERACTION between the representatives of the poor nations, who are mostly coloured, and the public of the richest nation, a minority of which is poor and coloured, provides most of the daily burden of the sacred drama. In the background always is the fear of world war, and it is the immensity of this fear, and of humanity's desire to avert it, that makes this place a sacred one, hallowed by the invocation of the victors in the last world war. But rare, fortunately, has been the kind of crisis in which men turn towards the United Nations as to a shrine and talisman for the averting of imminent doom. There have been only three such occasions—involving four crises—since the Korean war: the double crisis over Suez and Hungary in 1956; the Cuban missile crisis in 1962 and the Middle Eastern crisis of 1967 (which however was not of the same order of gravity as the others as no major power was *directly* involved). And in all four crises the United Nations provided all it had to provide: dramatised legitimation, an aura of dignity and piety, for the clothing of a great power which wanted to climb down, and whose climbing down preserved the peace. Thus, officially, Britain and France obeyed the resolution of the General Assembly when they withdrew from Egypt: officially, the United States was prevented by her commitments under the Charter, and by the 'Soviet veto' in the Security Council, from coming to the aid of Hungary; officially, the Soviet Union turned back its ships from their Caribbean course at the request of the Secretary-General. In the somewhat different circumstances of the Middle Eastern crisis, the Soviet Union was able to compensate—by vigorous use of the dramatic resources of the United Nations—for its non-intervention in a local struggle which ended in the defeat of its protégés.

The United Nations at such times performs the function of providing great powers with an alternative and sacrosanct means of preserving their dignity on the world stage in conditions where the normal means of preserving dignity, that of adhering to a consistent course, would carry them and the world over the brink of war. When one considers how large a part ideas of dignity and prestige have played among the origins of past wars, it is clear that this function of the United Nations, resting as it does on fiction and pretence, is none the less a real and vital safeguard of our survival.

In times of lesser tension, however, race is more prominent than other threats to peace in the performance of the United Nations.

The President of the Third Session of the General Assembly, Herbert Evatt, said that 'the United Nations is the temple of peace and the tribunal of justice'.[1] The relations between peace

Peace on Earth.

and justice are never easy: the wrangling before the tribunal is liable to disturb the service of the temple. The most disturbing of the demands for justice, those which are most menacing to peace, are those resulting from the application of racial laws. These are situations of a different kind from those great-power confrontations, in which the United Nations has been uniquely a safeguard of peace. Where the confrontations concerned are not between great powers, but between branches of the human race, and especially between black and white—involving the oppression of black by white—the tendency of the majority of the United Nations is to pursue justice, at some risk of war. Not that this language is used. The United Nations is by definition composed of its founder members plus 'the other peace-loving states'; the original peace-loving states were those which had won the war; the Korean war was fought under the 'Uniting for Peace' resolution; any future situation in which the United Nations may legitimise recourse to war will be designated as a threat to the peace, and made the object of a peace-keeping operation. The situation in Rhodesia has already been designated a threat to the peace. That in South-West Africa, as we have seen, may also be so designated, and the demand for a peace-keeping operation may not be capable of being resisted indefinitely. And a peace-keeping operation in Southern Africa would involve a local war on a considerable scale, because it would involve fighting the well-armed, well-trained and determined forces of the Republic of South Africa.

A well-informed observer, Mr Peter Calvocoressi, wrote in 1962: 'There are cases in which U.N. action is so dangerous as to be all but inconceivable. The outstanding example is a conflict which ranges blacks against whites. The U.N. could hardly intervene in such a quarrel without running the risk of destroying itself.'[2] The dangers perceived by Mr Calvocoressi are real, but so are the human pressures tending to involve the United Nations in such actions. The conflict in Katanga—in fact though not in legal form—was one that ranged blacks against whites—and the United Nations action there was bitterly opposed by almost all the local whites and their friends throughout the world. Sanctions against Rhodesia are a means of intervening in a black-against-white struggle. And the Rhodesian and South-West African situations point in the direction of sanctions against South Africa, and the possibility of eventual military action.

If this should come about, it will be as a result of the interplay between the Soviet Union, China, the United States, and the Afro-Asian countries generally. This interplay, if it occurred

[2] *World Order and New States: Problems of Keeping Peace*, p. 92.

in 'the real world' only, would be likely to lead to a *slow* build-up of pressure on South Africa. But the dramatisation and moralisation of the interplay, on the stage of the United Nations, speed up the process in the real world. The playing out of the roles, before the gallery, evokes a need to sustain them into real life; the actor's reputation, in his off-stage life, will affect his reception on his next public appearance; glory demands consistency. Now it is South Africa's misfortune—a richly-earned misfortune—that on this stage it is inescapably cast in the role of villain. In terms of the morality publicly professed by all the other participants, its actions cannot be defended. In a drama in which the actor's desire for glory reflects his conception of his role, nobody wants to be seen hobnobbing with the villain. Everyone becomes, on-stage, a little more anti-South African than he had been off-stage, and in each new performance South Africa becomes more odious. African delegates, who dislike South Africa to start with, grow more indignant as they hear themselves speak, and realise the moral power of what they symbolise. Soviet delegates, anxious to enhance their country's influence in the world at the expense of both America and China, try to be even more anti-South-African than the Africans. United States delegates, anxious to avert 'extreme' anti-South-African courses, are forced, in arguing accordingly, to protest that they abhor villainy as much as anyone, and find themselves obliged, in order to avoid 'the worst'—in terms of some immediate, concrete measure—to speak words, and give pledges for the future, which are likely to increase the pressure on South Africa and take the action of the play nearer to a final confrontation. The action, however, will be as long-drawn out as the behind-the-scenes activities of the United States and its Western European allies can make it. Yet the Soviet Union may have the power, in certain circumstances (as we have seen, pp. 24–8) and perhaps also the will, to speed up the action drastically. And if so the United States, caught in its role, might even have to follow.

That the 'limitations of the Charter' need not inhibit policy choices unless important Members want them to is shown by many instances (Korea, Congo, Dominican Republic, Vietnam, etc.). Article 51 of the Charter ('the right of self-defence') in practice recognises for each permanent member of the Security Council the right to use force whenever it considers its vital interests are affected. But the part played, and the lines spoken, in the theatre of the Charter are another matter, and do imply certain inhibitions on policy choices. The role, having to be resumed at an indefinite number of future performances, becomes an element in policy.

According to Auden:

> *Private faces in public places*
> *Are wiser and nicer*
> *Than public faces in private places.*

The faces that most concern us here are public faces in public places. These are under an obligation to seem as wise and as nice as they can. And if it is before an international public they are appearing then it is on that public's terms that they must try to appear wise and nice. Before an audience that abhors racism they must show abhorrence of racism. For Americans, before a United Nations public, this presents a special difficulty. It is easy enough for their delegates on the podium of the Assembly to abhor racial oppression with a moral fervour histrionically equivalent to John Brown's. But the United Nations audience in Manhattan can also contemplate other spectacles: that of Manhattan itself, with what Harlem represents in it and—on television and in the press—the American national spectacle, with what the South, and also the other big-city ghettoes represent in it. They have often watched these other spectacles with a sense of outrage and of shock. American delegates assure them that American policy is truly what they announce it to be, and that the American government fully shares their concern. They ask to see more evidence of this concern—and sometimes they see it. There is good reason to think that when President Eisenhower sent in Federal troops to Little Rock, Arkansas, in 1957, he was decisively influenced by the impact which reports and pictures from Arkansas were making on delegates to the United Nations General Assembly, then in session. The effort to sustain 'the credibility of the image' can lead to actions which would be incredible, if the image—in this case that of an anti-racist America—had not first been created and did not have to be sustained.

It was not created out of just nothing, and is not exclusively designed for foreigners. Many Americans, especially white middle-class women, really believe in it, and many more partly believe, or would like to believe. One may suspect also that 'the credibility of the image' is in certain circles a shame-faced cacophemism for virtue. A State Department official, for example, cannot, under 'off-stage' conditions, say—in writing a memorandum for the eyes of a superior—that to prevent coloured children going to school is wrong. Such language in such a context cannot be used, any more than the language of *realpolitik* can be used by an American diplomat on the public stage at the U.N. Both dialects—the virtuous public one and the tough one of the closed office—have something artificial and extravagant about them. The people concerned are not as idealist as they present themselves to the public, or as beady-eyed as they wish to seem to their colleagues and superiors, or as hypocritical as they might seem to anyone who had the opportunity to contrast the two sets of utterances (as happens, for example, whenever diplomatic archives are opened and contrasted with the public speeches of statesmen of the period). An official who —like an American U.N. delegate—has to use both dialects, may well prefer himself in his on-stage idealist persona to his beadiness of the memoranda. If so, he is certain to have recourse, in the beady language, to the 'credibility of the image', which must not be allowed to suffer. In so far as he himself is part of the image, his disinterestedness is less than perfect. But others, all of whose life and work is in the beady realm, have entered into a sort of uneasy collusion with the ethical by accepting and propagating the doctrine of the credible and inviolable image. In such cases, the world of fantasy invades the real world; the beady Frankenstein feels the grip of his idealist monster; the bureaucrats are stage-struck; fiction begins to turn into truth.

Mr Khrushchev, himself a vigorous performer on the buskined stage, used to like to tell the story of a questionnaire which the Bolsheviks, after their seizure of power, sent to all State employees. It included the question: 'Do you believe in God?' Knowing the views of their new masters, all but one of these civil servants answered 'no'. But there was among them, according to Khrushchev, just one honest man and he replied: 'In the office, no; at home, yes.' Many servants of powerful states—even officially God-fearing States—are in a similar position. For example, they may feel privately—'at home'—that oppression is wrong, but could never allow such ludicrous and unsound words to pass their lips before an office dictating machine. To pass from 'home' to 'office' God must put on the most unlikely disguise imaginable: that of the image of the State.

From a Nietzschean point of view—and really tough Western political thinkers are crypto-Nietzscheans—all this is sinister in the extreme. The strong, even though they may no longer believe in the slave-religion, are trapped by their lip-service to a slave-morality into doing the behests of an assembly of slaves—on Little Rock, in Katanga, towards Rhodesia. A sick white civilization is half in collusion with its black accusers, half ready to abandon or betray the outposts of the strong. Seen thus the drama may become *Samson Agonistes*—the hero blinded and reduced to the level of the slaves, with the catastrophe to come. American right-wing publicists—in such works as the Birchite *The Fearful Master*—seek to present a picture of this general kind. It is, of course, an exaggerated picture, but the fears it reflects are not ill-founded. The United States has far more influence over the United Nations than the Birchites imagine, but the continuing drama of the United Nations has more influence over the United States—mainly through the 'frozen role' and the 'sustained image'—than any American or European conservative can contemplate with anything less than deep disquiet. It is true that a great conservative, W. B. Yeats, wanted 'sacred drama' to become the 'first of the parables' but the kind of sacred drama he wanted was not international but national—'for all native eyes and ears'—and was to be acted out by strong farmers' sons in blue shirts, playing the parts of Fascist heroes, not very plausibly as it turned out. The sacred drama of the Assembly with its multicoloured cast, is necessarily very different. Its parable has never been continuously formulated—for its ambiguities have neither elegance nor even coherence—but it has something to do with peace and race and a deep connection between them. It seems to mean that without mutual respect among the branches of the human race there can be no safe peace. It seems also to mean that this respect is not likely to be universally achieved entirely by peaceful methods. And the white powers, in playing their roles within the drama, and acting up to them outside, have acquiesced in these suggestions to a greater extent than they intended, or than their peoples yet understand.

7

THE POWER of the weak over the strong is at best precarious and intermittent. The sacred drama may, in certain conditions, lose its power. It has, in fact, already lost some of it. 'The United Nations,' the British correspondent, Bernard Moore, pronounced as early as 1957 in *The Second Lesson*, 'is no longer fashionable.' It is certainly not more fashionable now than it was then. Its prestige in the poor world remains tarnished by association with the destruction of Lumumba; while Western opinion—little troubled by that—was shaken by its consequences, when the need to recover African confidence led to military action in Katanga and when the Secretariat, impelled by the need for verbal reconciliation between the new policy and the old, attempted to misrepresent the nature of this action (see *To Katanga and Back*, Chapter VI, 'The Fire in the Garage'). Its prestige was further lowered by the subsequent wrangle over the costs of the operation, when the United States attempt, using Article 19 of the Charter, to oblige the Soviet Union to pay 'its share' of the costs of the Congo operation, or lose its vote in the Assembly, prevented that body for a time from discharging its ritual functions. It is probable that nobody, anywhere, feels the same love and respect for the United Nations as many did in the 'forties and 'fifties.

Yet, although the audience has grown more critical, the drama is likely to continue, not for its aesthetic appeal—now quite small—but because of its ritual function. The Soviet Union, having neglected its share in the rites at the time of Korea, and seen the blessing and legitimising of the actions of an adversary, has experienced, in the Cuban missile crisis, the value of an institution, representing a superior moral power, before which one can incline to dignify a withdrawal. The Soviet Union has also now experienced, over the Middle East, just as the United States did over Hungary, the value of the United Nations in a situation where a policy of prudent but inglorious inaction has to be reconciled with an earlier posture of ostensible militancy. In the Middle Eastern crisis of 1967, the Soviet Union made a double use of the United Nations stage. First it used the Security Council to demonstrate its real resolve not to let the crisis escalate into a military confrontation of the great powers. This it did by calling, in concert with the United States, for a cease-fire. Next it used the United Nations to 'take the harm'—as we say in Ireland—out of its failure to support the Arab cause. This it did by having the General Assembly convened for a propaganda orgy, strongly reminiscent of the 'Hungarian' denunciation rituals of 1956, but with different objects of verbal immolation. Nor should it be assumed that the Soviet Government was notably chagrined by the 'defeat of its resolution'.

A defeat which could be plausibly and even accurately blamed on United States opposition may well have been almost as acceptable as an actual victory.[1] In any case it was the convening of the Assembly, combined with the tabling of the resolution and the speeches in its favour, that served the real Soviet purpose, which was to compensate for its failure to come to the aid of the Arab countries in the war, by dramatic demonstration in their favour after the war was over. And since popular opinion in Arab countries is widely believed to be not always quite clear about the existence of a distinction between rhetoric and reality, the compensation may well have been judged to be remarkably effective in proportion to its price—bearing in mind the relative costs of military action and of militant speeches.

As in the case of the Hungarian precedent and counterpart, the Soviet use of the United Nations in the Middle Eastern crisis sounds, when coldly described, sordid. No doubt, in both cases, those responsible took care not to see the matter in so cold a light themselves. And it must be remembered that in both cases the odd procedures thought necessary to save the face of a great power in a critical situation were helping thereby to safeguard world peace.

As the Middle Eastern debates in the Assembly illustrated, the Soviet position within the expanded and heavily 'anti-colonial' membership, is much less unfavourable now than it was for the first fifteen years of the life of the U.N. As the Soviet Union stoically endured so much moral obloquy during those years there is no reason why it should quit the United Nations now. The United States, for its part, seems unlikely to withdraw, leaving the Soviet Union in control of the machinery of legitimation. Strangely, the power which the United States has exercised—and still does weightily exercise, though in somewhat diminished degree—within the United Nations, has conferred on the United Nations some power over the United States. The American public has been brought up to believe that it believes in having 'a decent respect to the opinions of mankind'. American governments want to be thought of by that public in terms of what it has been brought up to believe that it believes, and there are signs that the public itself likes to think of its Government also in these terms. All this does not quite amount to actually having 'a decent respect to the opinions of mankind'—if it did, the war in Vietnam would be over long

---

[1] It is even possible that a strong resolution *defeated by the U.S.* was from the Soviet point of view a preferable outcome to the passage of such a resolution which might have raised hopes dangerously high. There are occasions when the Soviet and other delegations act as if they were heedful of the subtle diplomatic advice tendered by Pylade to Oreste in *Andromaque: Pressez, demandez tout, pour ne rien obtenir.*

since—but it does go far enough to support a vague respect for the version of the opinions of mankind presented on the East River. This is a version which American diplomatic, economic and military power has helped to shape, and therefore a version much more acceptable to the American public than any naked expression of foreign opinions would be likely to be. The spectacle on the East River may sometimes be disquieting, but it is more comforting than the news from the world at large.

One reason for this—in addition to unseen American influence over the other participants on the East River—is that America's own role at the United Nations seems—to viewer, listener or reader—to be pious and idealistic. The chief American representative at the United Nations is a sort of diplomatic television-bishop mediating between America's activities in the real world —which are no less hard and self-interested than those of other powers—and the ideas which America, in its church-going moods and aspects, likes to hold of itself. A Lodge, a Stevenson, a Goldberg, act out, for the American public, an ideal version of America's role in the world. In doing so they invoke the United Nations for a blessing on United States policy; if they cannot get the more-or-less real United Nations to go along, the *Platonic* United Nations can be made to serve. Mr Goldberg, for example, explained to an enthusiastic gathering in the Bronx on Washington's Birthday, 1967, that if the United States sometimes had to go it more or less alone—as in Vietnam—such things were necessary only until such time as the United Nations should be able to 'perform fully its role of peace-keeper'. Thus the action in Vietnam is not merely in accordance with the principles of the United Nations, but more in accordance with these principles than the actually existing United Nations is. This explanation is the more reassuring in that audiences of this kind are seldom altogether clear about the difference between a spokesman of the United States at the United Nations and a spokesman of the United Nations; the press itself often presents reports obviously emanating from the United States mission to the United Nations as if they came from 'the United Nations' itself.

The value of all this to any American administration, for the presentation of foreign affairs 'in correct perspective', needs no stressing. It is not an instrument which any administration could lightly relinquish. Yet it has its cost.

The putative blessing of the Platonic United Nations will do at a pinch for something—like the war in Vietnam or the invasion of Santo Domingo—for which the legitimation of the real General Assembly is not available. It is, however, a distinctly less consoling procedure: the wan and problematical approval of the distant, diluted God of the deists, as distinct from the comfort and satisfaction of the visible and audible correct performance of a rite. Mr Goldberg's audience on Washington's Birthday would have been much happier if he could have told it that the United States was carrying out in Vietnam the will of the United Nations, made known through a resolution of the General Assembly. A considerable part of the perplexity and uneasiness of American public opinion about the war in Vietnam —a state of opinion in marked contrast to the moral fervour behind the Korean war—comes from the fact that the rites have been neglected. They have been neglected perforce, because resolutions of the Korean and Hungarian type—resolutions precisely framed to meet the requirements of American policy —can no longer elicit the required two-thirds majority in the enlarged Assembly. The United States—either directly or through some other country—could of course bring the matter at any time before the Security Council, encounter the 'Soviet Veto' there and then take it into the Assembly with the 'Uniting for Peace' procedure established at the time of Korea. But it could not then get the required two-thirds, except for a draft negotiated with the Afro-Asians, and this would be either so vague as to be practically meaningless, or would constitute an encumbrance to the war effort. If the stage is reached when the United States wishes to prepare the way for a retreat from Vietnam, with as much dignity as possible, it may indeed resort to this precise procedure and 'bow to the United Nations'; up to now, still intent on a war policy, and lacking the votes for the blessing of this policy, it has kept the matter away from the United Nations, except for speeches, and the assumed benediction of the Platonic entity. But the American Government cannot explain this to its public.

The potential value of the United Nations as an instrument of national policy depends on a certain public haziness as to how it works. It must be thought of as benevolent, but not always in its right mind: capable of galvanic action but usually semi-paralysed; sometimes rallying to encourage the United States on some brave course (Korea); sometimes, through some strange inner weakness, from which it is doomed to suffer for a time, holding back the United States through the bonds of piety, from some other brave course (Hungary); and sometimes simply a silent and suffering victim here on earth, corresponding, however, to an avenging angel in Heaven, at whose behest, inaudible to others, the United States sets out on some brave course (Vietnam). This morality play, to be effective, must also be a mystery play. But, to have full ritual virtue, the play has to be acted out, and this is the weakness of versions which require the *Platonic* United Nations and cannot therefore be seen and heard. The uneasiness of the public—half-audience, half-congregation—is heard in such questions as: 'Why does the United Nations do nothing about Vietnam?' 'Why don't we *leave* it to the United Nations?' There are no answers to these questions which could satisfy the questioners, or leave them anything but either more perplexed, or more distressed.[2]

The United States then, cannot leave the actual United Nations, or reject the United Nations of its own public's imaginings. Being in, it has to strive to have the rituals conducted as nearly as possible in legitimation of its own policies. This requires it to influence votes in the Assembly, and this confers on the voters themselves some influence. And the fact that it is possible, through the United Nations, to exert some small influence over the policies of the greatest power on earth makes it practically worth while for other nations to keep up their membership—even if they were not also motivated, as they are, by honour and glory, the desire to shine and to be heard, or to be thought of at home as having shone and been heard. Many countries also have some special interest, some problem which they wish, not so much to solve, as to appear to be trying to solve. There are, on the one side, truths to be made known, world opinion to be aroused; on the other side there are calumnies to be refuted, world opinion to be adequately informed. Both sides know, or at any rate soon learn, that world opinion is profoundly indifferent to any local problem, unless it is also a white-versus-non-white racial problem, or unless the disputants can contrive to give it a turn involving the great powers, and thereby potentially menacing the continuance of human life. Few local (non-racial) disputants wish to arouse world opinion in this, the only efficacious, way. On the contrary, in bringing the problem before the United Nations, they are usually performing a ritual designed to appease those—including the ghosts of the ancestors—who clamour for material and drastic action. In racial cases—in Southern Africa, for example—the ritual has a graver significance and may be a legitimation of impending action. In other cases, however, the ritual is a substitute for action. The annual Arab immolation of the State

[2] At the time of writing, there are signs that the American Government may 'bring the matter to the United Nations' in order to dramatise its desire for peace, and also the absence of any alternative to its present policies. The only possible result of 'bringing the matter to the United Nations' in the absence of a desire on the part of the United States to change its policies will be a deadlock in the Security Council and an anodyne ('just peace') resolution of the General Assembly. The blessing of the United Nations could, however, be obtained and perhaps will be obtained by a future American President—for a change of policy, seriously aimed at actually getting out of Vietnam. This would have wide Afro-Asian—as well as Soviet bloc—support plus the Latin American and other faithful supporters of *all* United States policies. Such a combination of voting groups would come very close to unanimity.

of Israel in the years before the 1967 crisis was of this character. This sacrifice, offered up in the outward form of a debate on the Special Committee on the question of Palestine Refugees, was a symbolic fantasy entirely in the spirit of a spectacle organised by the Afro-Asian Youth Conference in Cairo:

'The high-light of the conference will be a large military manœuvre against Israel: 6,000 male students and 4,000 female students wearing the various uniforms of all Arab countries will participate in this little war. One group will represent the Israeli army. The programme gives the following description of the spectacle:

"All the Arab forces march towards Israel. The Israelis panic and take flight. In a victorious apotheosis the Israeli flag is torn down and replaced by the Arab flag." '[3]

The drawback of the New York ceremony, as distinct from the Cairo one, was that the Israelis failed to 'panic and take flight'. On the contrary, this annual drama, which brought emotional release to the Arabs, brought political and financial advantage to the Israelis. The Arabs were performing for their distant public in the Middle East, which heard their speeches on the radio, and read about them in the press, and no doubt derived satisfaction from their verbal excoriation of the enemy. But the Israelis were performing for New York television and reaching two publics of the greatest importance to them: the American Jewish public, and the American gentile public. To the Jewish public, the repeated Arab verbal onslaught brought annual confirmation that the State of Israel indeed remained in danger. This message was essential for the success of the mission of certain silent but important members of the Israeli delegation: the fund-raisers. (I remember a conversation with one of these, an elderly member of the Knesset. This gentleman approached me—I was then a member of the Irish delegation—about a singularly ill-inspired statement which a well-known Irish actress had just made on television. 'Is it true,' he asked, 'what Miss —— said, that Ireland is run by rich Jews?' I said no, there were few Jews in Ireland, and none of them really rich. I began to apologise for Miss —— but he cut me short. 'A pity,' he said. 'It is my job to look for rich Jews.') But the impact of the drama on the American non-Jewish public was also highly favourable from an Israeli point of view. The Arab speakers who were heard in this particular debate were very fierce and very foreign; their English was unusual, their style of oratory vigorous but strange. Israel, on the other hand, could always produce a protagonist with a command of English not less, and usually

[3] *La Depeche Tunisienne*, 1 February, 1959; quoted in Albert Memmi, *The Liberation of the Jew*.

IN ACTION
CONGO
MIDDLE EAST

The CONGO theme will be concluded in No. 1, 196

Congo
Leopoldville

Congolese soldiers & officer

Congo UN troops & Congolese soldiers

Belgian Nun
Congo
Stanleyville – Congolese Soldiers

Stanleyville Airport

Congo, Leopoldville

Abissinian UN Troops
Congo

2" width rest in pro →

ONU

2" width rest in pro →

Ruandi Urundi
Congo refugees and UN Irish troops

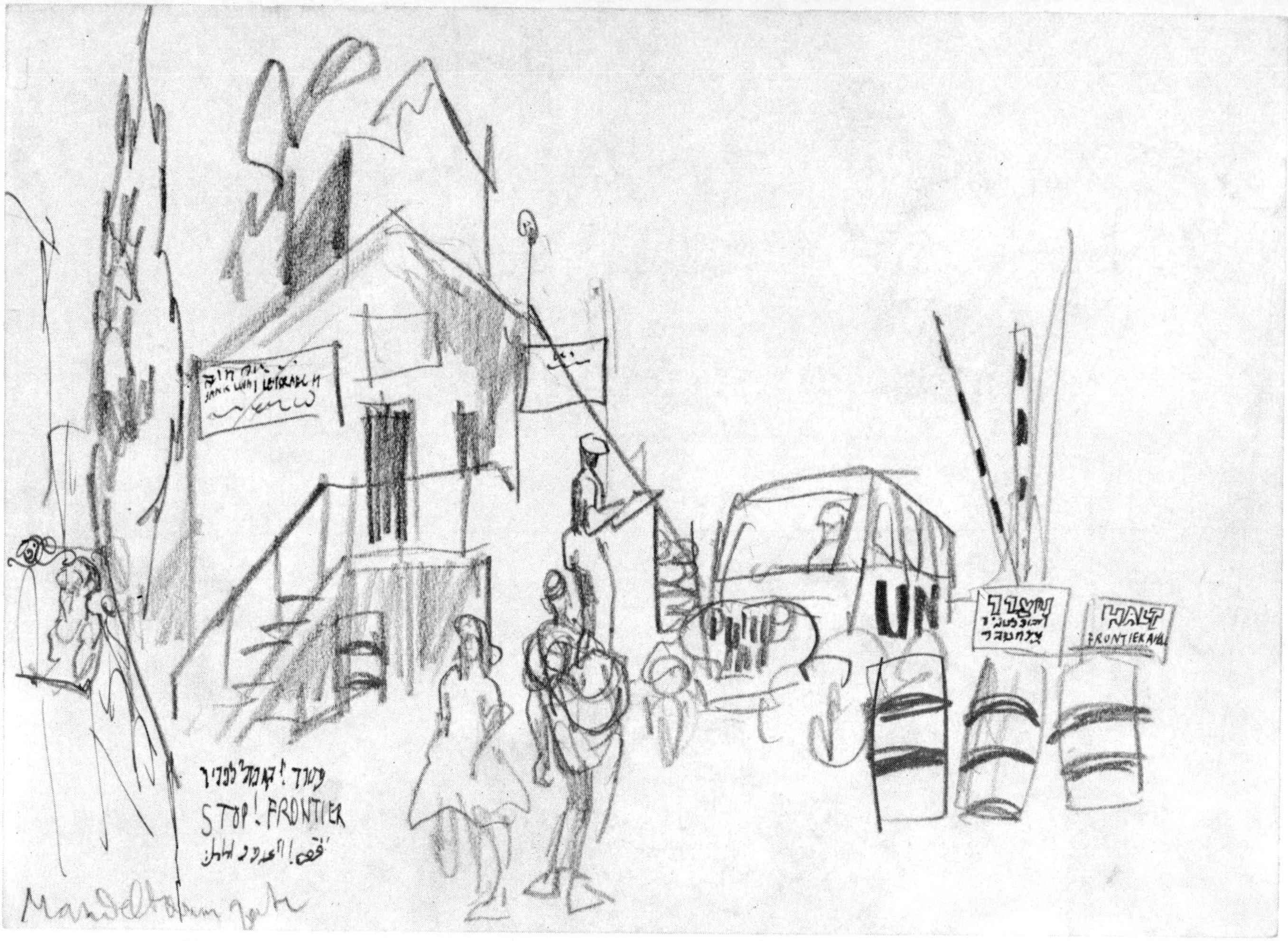
STOP! FRONTIER
UN
HALT
Mandelbaum gate

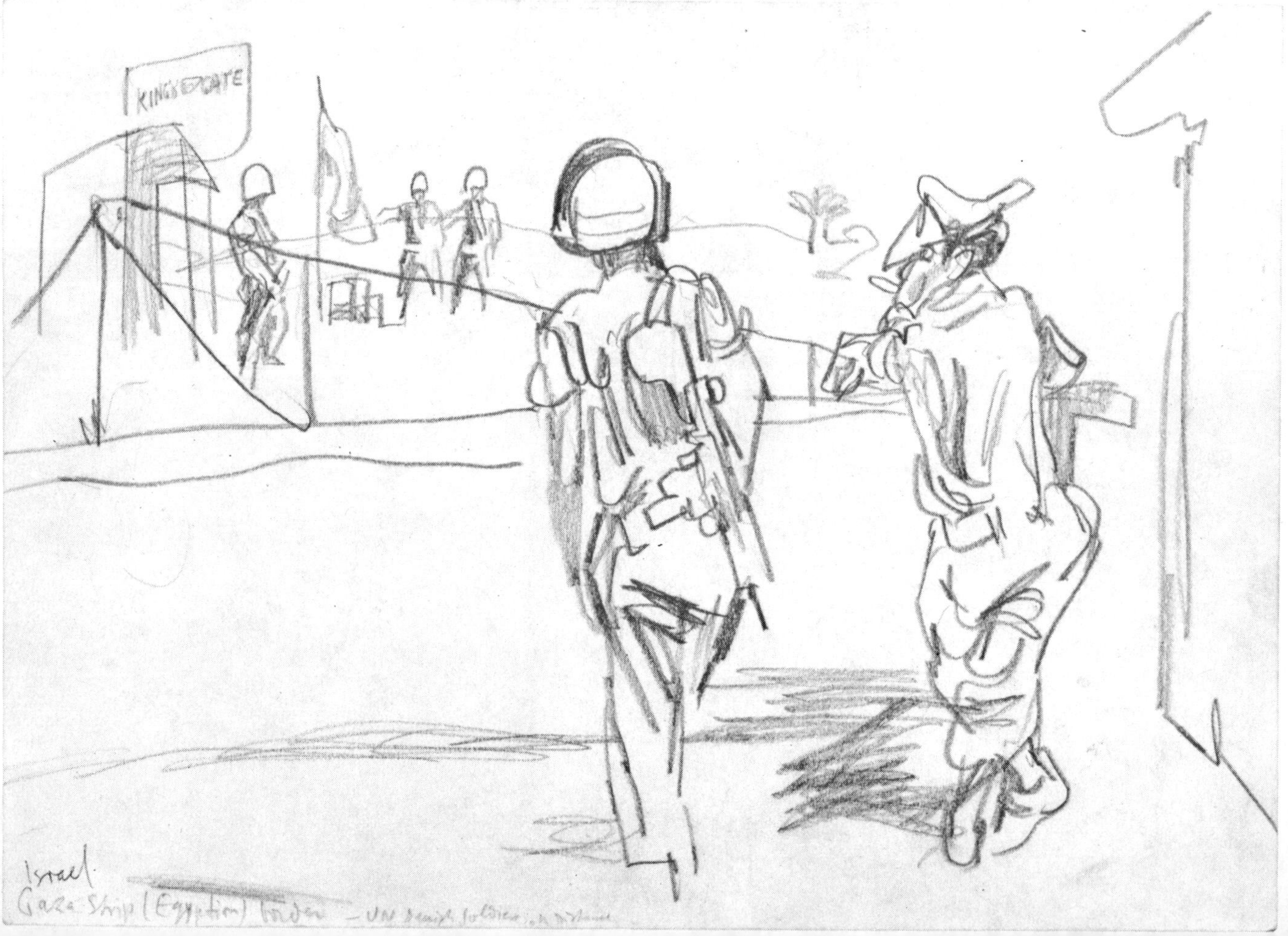
Israel.
Gaza Strip (Egyptian) border — UN Danish soldiers

Israel, Kibutz Ein-Gev. Night Watch at the Gates (Sabra: German-Russian) girl-soldier on the Sea of Galilee. Syrian border

greater, than that possessed by most British and American delegates, and an experienced readiness in debate not to be matched in any other delegation. He was likely to speak with studied restraint, emphasising Israel's desire for peace. His whole style was Western and measured, and an American audience —even one somewhat prejudiced against Jews and Israel— would be hard put to it not to identify him with the good guy, and his Arab adversaries with the Indians circling the covered wagon. The deeper implications of the analogy would be likely to be missed.

Things at the United Nations did not always go Israel's way, because there were factors in the real world—including strategic considerations, the politics of oil, America's supposed need to counter Communism in the Arab world—which ran against Israel. But as far as the working of the sacred drama is concerned, Jehovah did not let his people down, while Mahomet assumed the part of the foiled heavy, which was his in mediaeval plays.

This drama was, of course, based on two enormous tragedies, yet, as acted out at the United Nations, it had strong elements of comedy. These last were eclipsed during the 1967 crisis, which added yet another bloody and tragic scene. Yet the essential character of the drama did not change. The Arab states continued to 'act out' their hostility towards Israel, but this time they acted it out in such a way as to give Israel the pretext to strike them a crushing blow. They did this by a symbolic act accompanied by verbal menace. The symbolic act was the exorcising of a symbolic force—the United Nations Expeditionary Force. This small force had been stationed on Egyptian soil—with the consent of Egypt—in 1956, in order to 'act out' the achievement of the purpose of 'separating the combatants' which Britain and France pretended to have prompted their Suez intervention. (See pp. 12, 66, 222 and 284.) Being on Egyptian soil, and not on the soil of Israel, it was a living expression of the fact that Egypt, not Israel, needed to be protected. It was felt, therefore, by Arabs as a symbol of Egyptian weakness, and President Nasser acted to remove this symbol. In retrospect, it seems a great blunder to have removed the symbol without having changed the reality which it had represented.[4] The change was inevitably

---

[4] The blunder was President Nasser's. The criticism which has been directed against U Thant for complying with Nasser's request to remove the Force ignores a material fact linked to a juridical one. The material fact is that the Force was a very small one which could have been either expelled or—more probably—harassed and humiliated by the numerous and well-armed, though inefficient, Egyptian army. The juridical fact was that the Force was in Egypt not in virtue of a mandatory decision of the Security Council under Chapter VII of the Charter, but because of voluntary compliance, by Egypt and some other countries, with a recommendation of the General Assembly. An attempt by U Thant to keep the Force in Egypt, against the will of the Government by whose invitation it was there, would not have been supported by the Security Council, of which one Permanent Member denied that the Force in question was a properly constituted United

accompanied by a continuation of the usual verbal violence against Israel—a verbal violence which, however, inevitably now received much wider international coverage—and by various threats, notably that of closing the gulf of Aqaba to Israel shipping. For Nasser's Arab audience this was no doubt dramatically satisfying. But in reaching a wider audience it played—as previous Arab performances had done—into Israel's hands. Tiny Israel seemed in peril of her life, surrounded by these large and menacing neighbours: it had been 'deserted' by the United Nations, whose force, opinion in the West was rather apt to assume, was or should be there to protect Israel: the threat to the Gulf of Aqaba was represented as a threat to Israel's national existence, which was scarcely the case. Thus the drama which pleased the Arabs also provided the perfect *mise-en-scène* for Israel to do what it wanted—which was to use its efficient and brilliantly led armed forces to hit the Arabs very hard indeed—without incurring any great international opprobrium, in the countries where such opprobrium could do real damage. And when the short war was over, the continuation of the drama, on the old stage of the United Nations, served its old purposes—that of satisfying the feelings of the Arabs, and that of reminding friends of Israel that, whatever victories might be won, the State remained in danger and required support.

The ritual possibilities open to small countries for 'solving' their special problems for good or ill by acting them out are many and varied. They range from the faintest of indirect allusions to Schleswig-Holstein by a Danish delegate, to the tabling of a resolution by Austria, on the 'problem of Bolzano-Bozen'. (The problem is so designated officially by the United Nations in order not to appear to side with the Austrians by calling it South Tyrol, or with the Italians by calling it Alto-Adige.) The last method, the full and solemn ritual of a resolution leading to a vote, will often, for various reasons, not be found appropriate. A small country, wishing to resort to this, may, for example, be warned off by a larger power, usually the United States, or it may, independently, fear that the vote will be adverse, or contemptuously vague and perfunctory, and thereby not only exacerbate the problem, but also discredit the government which so maladroitly raised it. Or the government concerned may fear that the vote would be *too* favourable, arousing

---

Nations Force at all. Subsequent proceedings in the General Assembly do not suggest that a majority could have been found there for keeping the Force in Egypt, or for any other mandate. In the circumstances the most that can fairly be claimed by U Thant's critics is that by 'stalling' he might—at the price of an unknown amount of humiliation for the U.N. Force—have earned a limited amount of time. No one has shown any reason to believe that the time thus 'gained' would have been used for anything else but further 'let-me-at-'em' histrionics by Cairo Radio, and further political and military planning by Israel.

hopes and passions and leading to incalculable complications. Certain rituals can be a substitute for violence; others are such powerful medicine that they might lead to violence. It is, for this reason, I believe, that Ireland—nominally committed to arousing the conscience of the world to the injustice of partition—has never submitted a resolution on the subject to the United Nations, where it might well have got strong 'anti-colonialist' support, and blown the embers alight again.

No group of men had a better grasp of the power of sacred drama than those for whom Yeats's *Cathleen Ni Houlihan* had been, in the words of the late P. S. O'Hegarty, 'a sort of sacrament'. This was the play of which the dying Yeats asked himself:

> *Did that play of mine send out*
> *Certain men the English shot?*

The heirs of those men have deliberately refrained from summoning up the dramatising possibilities of the United Nations. Fearing these possibilities—very understandably, but contrary to their own rhetoric, resembling in this, on a small scale, the American Republicans on Hungary—they have avoided the grand ritual, and resorted to the petty one, the allusion in the speech, noticed at home and ignored abroad. But the possibility of recourse to the grand ritual remains in reserve—in this and other similar cases—and probably has a certain restraining influence on all the parties to the dispute.

The small countries then—the great bulk of the membership—have ample reasons for continuing to support 'their organisation'. The United States and the Soviet Union have adequate reasons for doing so. The smaller great powers, Britain and France, have on the whole a more chilly attitude, though Britain, under a Labour Government, may sometimes find 'support for the United Nations' a virtuous formula to cover support accorded, on financial grounds, to the United States. (Supporters of the British Labour Government's foreign policy must regret that the General Assembly could not have been persuaded to legitimise America's war in Vietnam, thereby not only consoling the American public, but providing Mr. Wilson with a much-needed moral umbrella.) But whether they treat the United Nations with open contempt, as France has done, or—as Britain usually does—with sanctimonious respect over-acted for an American public, they cannot very well keep out of it, as long as the United States, the Soviet Union and the Afro-Asians stay in. Otherwise the competition between the superpowers for Afro-Asian support endangers the interests of Britain and France to an even greater extent than it does now. If these nations do not act their own parts, leaving only the others to be acted, the play will become even more ominous. In the last resort, everyone must stay in for fear of everyone else.

The sacred drama, then, seems likely to continue, even though it is usually ill-performed and often incomprehensible, and even though sections of the public grow bored or disillusioned, object or wander away. Other sacred and theatrical centres have had their ups and downs, their hours of glory, their ludicrous and ignominious moments and their humdrum years, and yet lived long enough to become venerable monuments in the history of civilisation. The United Nations may be regarded as continuing, in this modern world in which religious awe is attenuated and diffused, some of the principal functions of the mediaeval Vatican, and of the shrine of Delphi in classical times.

8 As REGARDS the Vatican, the parallel occurred to Hammarskjold himself, against a dramatic and sacrificial imaginative background. In public, he repudiated such a concept. 'We are no Vatican', he told the United Nations Correspondents Association just before the beginning of his second term of office. In private conversation he was not quite so sure: 'To be Secretary-General of the United Nations,' writes W. H. Auden in the Foreword to *Markings*—'he once jokingly told me is like being a secular Pope and the Papal throne is a lonely eminence.' There is no joke at all, in his private notations, about his conception of the divine purpose behind the United Nations, and of his own role, combining that of high-priest and victim, essentially the idea of Christ's Vicar re-enacting the sacrifice of Christ. 'You are dedicated to this task,' he wrote in his diary in 1955—'because of the Divine intention behind what is, in fact, only a sacrificial rite in a still barbarian cult: a feeble creation of man's hands— but you have to give your all to this human dream for the sake of that which alone gives it reality.'[1] About five years later—apparently at the time of the Soviet and other attacks on him over the Congo—he is sure that the victim in the sacrificial rite is himself:

> *I have watched the others:*
> *Now I am the victim*
> *Strapped fast to the altar*
> *For sacrifice.*
>
> *Dumb, my naked body*
> *Endures the stoning, dumb*
> *When slit up and the live*
> *Heart is plucked out.*

It is certain that Hammarskjold thought of himself as the central figure in a sacred drama: king, pontiff, victim. He wrote in 1957: 'Oedipus the son of a king [Hammarskjold's father had been Prime Minister of Sweden], the winner of a throne, fortunate and innocent, is compelled to recognise the possibility and in the end the fact that he, too, is guilty, which makes it just that he should be sacrificed to save the city.'[2]

The governments which in 1953 agreed on the choice of Dag Hammarskjold as Secretary-General presumably imagined that they were picking a cautious, neutral Civil Servant, not a sacrificial victim. As those who arranged the election of Popes so often did, they got more than they bargained for. It is probably inevitable that this should be so. When the United States and

[1] *Markings*, 110.
[2] Ibid, 114.

the Soviet Union agree on the choice of a candidate it is likely that someone is making a mistake, and there will be times when both are doing so.

But the qualities have first to be there, even if unsuspected. It may be, of course, that the role of Secretary-General actually changed the man. 'Often,' says Professor Michael Banton, 'a role brings out in individuals qualities that might otherwise have gone unsuspected (the late Dag Hammarskjold and former President Truman are only two among many reputed examples of this)'.[3] There is no evidence that either the first Secretary-General, Trygve Lie, or the third, U Thant, ever thought of himself as a secular Pope, or a sacrificial victim. Lie, indeed, showed an interest in the theatrical side of his office, but only in a profane, show-business sort of way. His book, *In the Cause of Peace*, reveals a mind as commonplace as the most cautious of politicians could wish a Civil Servant to possess. Thant, shy, tentative, and in his early years of office almost inarticulate, is the reverse of theatrical, though he is religious.

It is not, I think, an accident that the most eminent and impressive of the Secretaries-General should also have been the most fantastic. It is because the functions of the United Nations are sacred and dramatic that Hammarskjold was particularly fitted to serve it. He had style, imagination, and a deep sense of the religious importance of his office: qualities far more important than 'organising ability' for this particular 'organisation'. He was also something of an actor, knew it and scolded himself for it: 'Vanity rears its ridiculous little head and holds up the distorting mirror in front of you. For an instant the play actor adjusts his smile and his features to the role. For a mere instant—but one too many. It is at such times that you invite defeat and betray Him whom you serve.'[4] The 'for a mere instant' is unconvincing. The man who is in the habit of using the second person about himself in his diary is clearly an attentive spectator of his own actions: so high a degree of self-consciousness implies that acting will be among the actions. A former close associate of Hammarskjold's spoke of him (in private) as a narcissist, and said that as soon as he became friendly with anyone, he became jealous of that person's friendship with himself, and had to sever that relation. I was inclined to be sceptical about this observation, regarding it as perhaps too ingenious to be true, but a reading of *Markings* makes it more plausible. The 'vanity' passage for example may be interpreted as implying irritation at the fact that he had permitted himself to play for a wider audience than the intimate one represented

[3] *Roles*, p. 100.
[4] *Markings*, 144.

by the diarist. As far as the service of the United Nations was concerned, however, the irritation was misplaced, for the acting was part of the service, not a distraction from it. By his style and demeanour, more than by any single thing he actually did, Hammarskjold projected the sense that the United Nations was extremely important. This priest induced in the believer, and even in some former unbelievers, the feeling that the rites, having been duly celebrated, were valid and binding. The sacred authority of the shrine was reinforced and therefore the political activity around the shrine increased, bringing with it a further accession of authority. If he was a secular Pope, he was a great one. Yet great Popes have not always left the Church stronger than they found her, and the United Nations, after Hammarskjold, was diminished in repute and in authority. As with the Popes, the trouble stemmed from a conflict between charisma and the temporal power. And here it is necessary to say something about the temporal power, not of the United Nations—for it has none—but of the Secretary-General in his role as peacekeeper.

Stalin's enquiry is well known: 'How many divisions has the Pope?' For the Secretary-General of the United Nations the answer is normally the same as for the Pope today: none. As the Military Staff Committee provided for in Article 47 of the Charter never came into effective being, international enforcement action, in the sense contemplated in the Charter (in Chapter VII) never came about. Those who framed the Charter and its Chapter VII had been thinking in terms of machinery for renewed combined action by the Allies against any revival of German or Japanese military power. With the onset of the Cold War, international relations took on a different shape and the Military Staff Committee became a dead letter.

None the less, the Secretary-General may, in certain circumstances, have at least some degree of control over military forces, or say in their disposition. This fact, more than any other, has confused public opinion about the United Nations, by creating the illusion that somehow it does have 'real power' at its disposal if it cares to use it. After all, if it can 'act' in Korea or in the Congo why does it have to be powerless in other instances? The fact remains that the United Nations, in itself—Article 47 being a dead letter—has no material power at all: only the spiritual power of blessing the actions of others. Yet, as the result of its blessing, its Secretary-General may become involved in decisions affecting the application of material force. And in so doing he may gravely impair his spiritual authority, in the same way as the Popes impaired theirs by the momentum of their temporal power.

Thus the first two Secretaries-General were led to undermine their own authority, in the course of the two main 'peace-keeping' efforts legitimised by the United Nations: Lie on Korea, Hammarskjold on the Congo. These two operations varied widely, but they led to one identical conclusion: the repudiation of the Secretary-General by that superpower which has less influence in the United Nations than the other—but may have enough power, all the same, to destroy human life on the planet. Repudiation by one of the superpowers means the end of the Secretary-General as high-priest of the shrine of survival. He can no longer mediate, solemnly entreat, make holy the paths of withdrawal. He can only press dourly ahead, amid shouts of hatred from at least one side, at a 'peace-keeping' mission which he knows will be the last entrusted to him. A Hammarskjold bogged down in the Congo resembles an Innocent III squandering the spiritual resources of his office and his mind in desperate efforts to restore the status quo in the Marches of Ancona and Spoleto.

It is the contention of the present writer that it is both possible and urgently necessary to restore and safeguard the spiritual authority of the Secretary-General, and that this can only be ensured by taking responsibility for peace-keeping operations away from him. These things must sometimes come, as a lesser evil, but woe unto him through whom they come. Peace-keeping operations involve at least the danger of bloodshed; great bloodshed in Korea, some in the Congo. And military operations, and the diplomacy required to sustain them, will entail the use of ruse and stratagem, that is to say, of lying. Now soldiers may kill, and diplomats may lie, without having done what they are not expected to do, and therefore without impairing their effectiveness. But priests are expected (today at least) to be above lying to people, or killing them, and above all the custodian of a shrine of survival must be thought of as being above these things. The only way to be securely so thought of is to refrain, not only from the direct commission of these acts, but from having responsibility for their commission by others. *This necessitates the absolute avoidance of responsibility for the conduct of any military operation whatsoever,* no matter how excellent its purpose, and even if it is blessed by the Security Council and the General Assembly. It is fundamentally wrong, in view of the religious nature of the United Nations, to regard its Secretary-General as just a diplomat and administrative functionary to whom mundane tasks may be assigned by the Security Council (or Assembly) just as national Governments assign tasks—often involving some measure of the sordid or the brutal—to their servants. This is wrong, because the United

Nations, having no authority save a religious and moral one, loses much of its utility for our survival if it or its chief servant is seen to behave as great powers can behave, whose authority, whatever they may claim, is neither religious nor moral, but material.

Before discussing how the spiritual authority of the Secretary-General may be protected in any future peace-keeping operations, it is necessary to consider briefly in what ways this authority became compromised in the two very different major operations —Korea and the Congo—which have already taken place.

On 25 June, 1950, the armed forces of North Korea invaded South Korea. The United States Government requested the Secretary-General [Mr Trygve Lie] to convene an immediate meeting of the Security Council, and he did so.

The members of the Security Council, without the Soviet Union, which was then boycotting meetings because of the continued seating in China's place of a Kuomintang delegation in the place of the government actually controlling the Chinese mainland, met on 25 June. The President—by previous arrangement according to Mr Lie's memoirs[5] called on the Secretary-General to speak first. Mr Lie spoke briefly but, as he says, 'with emphasis'. He concluded with the words:

'The present situation is a serious one and is a threat to international peace. The Security Council is, in my opinion, the competent organ to deal with it.

'I consider it the clear duty of the Security Council to take steps necessary to re-establish peace in that area.'[6]

On this, in his memoirs, he makes two significant glosses: first, that his statement that the Security Council was 'the competent organ' was a 'legal opinion' which he advanced 'in spite of and in opposition to the Soviet contention that the Security Council was not competent to act because of the presence of the "Kuomintang clique" and the absence of representatives of the U.S.S.R. and the Chinese Communist government'; and second, that by his assertion about 'the clear duty of the Security Council' he 'anticipated and associated my office and myself with the most determined effort to give reality to the principles of collective security'.[7]

Mr Lie's conception—certainly in retrospect and possibly at the time—was that he was acting under Article 99 of the Charter, under which the Secretary-General 'may bring to the attention of the Security Council any matter which in his opinion may threaten the maintenance of international peace and

---

[5] *In the Cause of Peace*, p. 329.
[6] *Security Council Official Records, Fifth Year, 473rd meeting.*
[7] *In the Cause of Peace*, p. 330.

security'. Mr Lie made this claim before the General Assembly three months later, when he referred to 'my statement to the Security Council on 25 June last concerning the Korean conflict when for the first time I invoked Article 99 of the Charter'.[8] Members of the Security Council may, however, not have been aware, on that momentous 25 June, that Article 99 was being invoked. The matter was 'brought to the attention' of the Security Council, not by the Secretary-General but by the United States, and the first item on the agenda of the Council was a letter 'from the representative of the United States of America addressed to the Secretary-General transmitting a communication to the President of the Security Council covering an act of aggression upon the Republic of Korea'.[9] The Secretary-General did not claim the floor under Article 99; he was called on by the President to state whether he had any 'interim reports' from the United Nations Commission then in Korea. The Secretary-General did not explicitly refer to Article 99 in his remarks, and the only basis there can be for the claim that he 'invoked Article 99 for the first time' is the fact that he used the words 'threat to international peace' in a statement which 'by previous arrangement with the President' he managed to get in before the United States representative spoke.

The retrospective significance of the dubious claim that Article 99 was invoked is that the myth of Korea as a United Nations 'collective security' action (rather than a United States action blessed by part of the Security Council and by the General Assembly) is thereby strengthened. The significance of the Secretary-General's intervention *at the time*—and in particular his reference to 'the competent organ'—was that it strengthened the United States claim that members of the Security Council, *without the Soviet Union*, were competent to take major decisions, *as the Security Council*.

The Charter states in Article 27(3) that: 'Decisions of the Security Council on all [non-procedural] matters shall be made by an affirmative vote of seven members including the concurring votes of the permanent members' . . . (exceptions are mentioned, not, however, relevant to action under Chapter VII, which was involved here). Mr Lie's 'legal opinion' was therefore contrary to the literal meaning of the Charter, as well as to the known intentions of the founders.[10] It is clear, however, that it was not

---

[8] *General Assembly Official Records, Fifth Session, 289th meeting*—28 September, 1950.

[9] *Security Council Records, 473rd meeting.*

[10] Mr Lie later 'circulated privately among key delegations and persons' a memorandum prepared by the Legal Department, according to which 'The absence of the USSR in accordance with United Nations practice did not constitute an automatic veto of substantive resolutions then adopted; rather it was equivalent to an abstention.' (I.C.P., p. 335). The Soviet case of course was that forms of

of decisive importance whether or not the Security Council was competent to act, or even whether or not it 'acted'. On 25 June, its members who were present adopted, or purported to adopt, a resolution submitted by the United States, calling for the immediate cessation of hostilities and the withdrawal of the North Korean forces and 'calling upon all members to render every assistance to the United Nations in the execution of this resolution'. As a mandate for intervention, this was rather vague. A Security Council meeting was summoned for the morning of 27 June to consider a more specific proposal. The meeting had to be postponed until the afternoon, however, and the United States was not prepared to wait, even for a few hours, for a clear (though possibly illegal) mandate. 'Because of the delay in the Security Council meeting,' writes Mr Lie, 'the President thus ordered American forces into action before the Council adopted, the same evening, a resolution which recommended that "the members of the United Nations furnish such assistance to the Republic of Korea as may be necessary to repel the armed attack and to restore international peace and security in the area".'[11] Mr Lie makes it clear that, even if this retrospective clarion-call had not sounded from (part of) the Security Council, it would have sounded, with equal effect, from the Assembly. Before the (putatively critical) afternoon meeting of 27 June, Mr Lie attended a luncheon at which the Soviet delegate, Yakov Malik, and the United States deputy representative, Ernest Gross, were both present. 'As we came to dessert and coffee,' writes Mr Lie, 'I recalled to Mr Malik that the rest of us were about to set off to the meeting of the Security Council. "Won't you join us? The interests of your country would seem to me to call for your presence." He shook his head and replied: "No, I will not go there!"

'Ernest Gross and I walked out together and got into my car. His relief that Mr Malik had not come was unconcealed. "Think," he said with considerable feeling, "what would have happened if he had accepted your invitation." I responded: "Yes, it would have been difficult. We would have had to fight it out, and move on to the General Assembly." '[12]

Mr Lie then tried to get into his hands as much responsibility as he could for the conduct of the Korean war. 'The Secretary-General,' he writes, 'very frequently is the executive for the decisions by the legislative organs of the United Nations, and

---

U.N. 'practice' which were contrary to the wording of the Charter, and to which the Soviet Union objected, were a violation of the Charter. The distinction here between *abstention*—implying a degree of assent to a known proposition—and *absence* is obvious.

[11] *In the Cause of Peace*, p. 332.
[12] Ibid, p. 333.

this was my role in the Korean conflict.'[13] It was certainly the role he sought, but his actual role in executing the decisions of the 'legislative organs' was distinctly less important that than of General McArthur. He attempted to set up a 'Committee on Co-ordination of Assistance for Korea', of which he would have been Rapporteur. On this the 'United States Mission promptly turned thumbs down'[14] and Mr Lie had to content himself with attaching a South African liaison officer to General MacArthur, getting the Chief of Staff of the United States Army to present a United Nations flag to General MacArthur, and sending telegrams to member nations asking them to try to provide 'an increased volume of combat forces, particularly ground forces' to be placed under the Unified Command, that is, General MacArthur.

Mr Lie also went so far as to propose the formation of an international brigade 'which would be organised by the United States, but at the disposal of the Security Council'; 'the only practical way of organising the brigade was to entrust the responsibility—and the expense—to the United States'.[15] This idea was too much for the United States representatives themselves, and was therefore dropped, like the Co-ordinating Committee with its Rapporteur.

In August, Mr Malik (Soviet Union) returned and took the chair of the Security Council, and the Council therefore ceased to be available (because of the veto) for further legitimations of the American intervention. Accordingly, the General Assembly became the theatre for these rites. The United States induced the General Assembly to adopt, on 3 November, 1950, a procedure designed to 'bypass the veto'—and thereby the original intent of the founders of the United Nations. This was the procedure, known as 'Uniting for Peace' under which the General Assembly resolved: 'that if the Security Council because of lack of unanimity of the permanent members, fails to exercise its primary responsibility for the maintenance of international peace and security in any case where there appears to be a threat to the peace, breach of the peace or act of aggression, the General Assembly shall consider the matter immediately with a view to making appropriate recommendations to members for collective measures, including in the case of a breach of the peace or act of aggression the use of armed force when necessary, to maintain international peace and security. . . .'

Vyshinsky, in commenting on this draft resolution, drew attention, with the help of the American magazine, *Newsweek*,

[13] *In the Cause of Peace*, p. 333.
[14] Ibid, p. 334.
[15] Ibid, p. 339.

to the essentially dramatic character of these transactions:

'This article [an article in *Newsweek* for 18 September, 1950] says that the motive of the United States in submitting this plan to the Assembly was that the situation called for the adoption of dramatic rather than legal action. In other words there is no need to consider the legal position or the law of our Organisation —the Charter—if the circumstances require that it should not be considered. That I understand: that is an honest way of putting the question. But then you, the authors of the draft resolution, should have said: "Yes, it is a breach of the Charter, but the position is such that we have to break that Charter. It is the dramatic situation which obliges us to act in this way, not legal considerations. Legal considerations must give way before the dramatic circumstances which have arisen." If you had done that, we should at any rate have had no quarrel with you. We should then have had to decide on our position in an organisation of that kind. We should have given it our consideration.'[16]

The speaker's record gives an extra dimension of irony to his remarks. The former chief prosecutor at the Moscow Trials was, after all, one of the greatest living connoisseurs of situations in which 'legal considerations must give way before the dramatic circumstances'.

As the United States at this time had a safe two-thirds majority in the Assembly, this was at the time a procedure for instant legitimation of whatever the United States wanted—although, in the long term, it was also, as Mr Lie rightly says, 'a shift the full potentialities of which have still to be realised'.[17] Mr Lie, who regarded 'Uniting for Peace' as 'a profoundly important shift of emergency power from the veto-ridden Security Council to the veto-less General Assembly' is proud of having abetted this shift: 'I publicly indicated my support for the plan while it was being debated and, once it was adopted, I appointed a special co-ordinating committee of senior Secretariat members to advance the implementing of the resolution.'[18]

In short, the Charter, as originally conceived, was bypassed at this time in the interests of the power with the greatest influence in the principal organs of the United Nations, and the Secretary-General co-operated in this process, with an enthusiasm which sometimes even exceeded the wishes of the power in question.

It is in no way surprising that Trygve Lie, as Secretary-General, should have become *persona non grata* to the Soviet Union. He played, according to Mr Gromyko, 'an unseemly

---

[16] *General Assembly, Fifth Session; 301st meeting:* 2 November, 1950.
[17] *In the Cause of Peace*, p. 347.
[18] Ibid, p. 347.

role' having 'obsequiously helped a gross violation of the Charter on the part of the United States Government and other members of the Security Council'.[19]

Mr Lie's term of office ended in November 1950. The Charter provides (Article 97) that 'the Secretary-General shall be appointed by the General Assembly upon the recommendation of the Security Council'. The Charter also states, as we have seen, that decisions of the Security Council, on all matters other than procedure, require 'the concurring votes of the permanent members'. In the Security Council the Soviet Union voted against Mr Lie's reappointment. The United States, however, continued to support Mr Lie; it was said, rather absurdly, that the United States would use the veto against any other candidate. There was never any danger of the United States being in a minority in the Security Council, and the concept of 'the veto'—a negative vote by a permanent member invalidating a decision which the Council would otherwise have taken—was therefore hardly relevant. The Soviet Union made clear its position, that 'if the appointment of Mr Lie is imposed, the USSR will not take Mr Lie into account and will not consider him as Secretary-General of the United Nations'. None the less, Mr Lie continued in office, relying on a vote in his favour in the General Assembly, *without* a recommendation from the Security Council, and without the recognition of one of the permanent members. It was not, as Mr Lie himself allows, 'a happy state of affairs'. Even some undeviating supporters of the United States expressed their reservations about this transaction, in that dialect of philosophic uncertainty in which alone such reservations can be expressed. 'Whether the General Assembly,' said General Romulo of the Philippines, 'without any recommendation from the Security Council can extend Mr Lie's term for three years is a fine point of law which has fascinated many.'[20]

From the point of view of the United States Government, however, this possibly illegal extension had at that time its advantages. This Secretary-General discharged from United Nations service a number of American nationals on the sole ground that they had availed themselves, in American domestic proceedings, of an American constitutional right—which Mr Lie calls a privilege—by pleading the Fifth Amendment. 'The exercise of the constitutional privilege under American Law,' said Mr Lie, 'does not imply any similar constitutional right to public employment by the one who exerts it.'[21] So he fired them,

[19] *In the Cause of Peace.*
[20] *297th meeting:* 31 October, 1950.
[21] *In the Cause of Peace*, p. 396.

and also permitted the F.B.I. to install its investigators within the Secretariat building, and to process international civil servants for the intensity of their loyalty to a particular nation, as measured by the criteria of the McCarthy era.

Mr Lie speaks of 'the atmosphere of Greek tragedy that pervaded the whole affair',[22] but in fact United Nations theatre in his day was not on that level; it was more like the black buffoonery of *Ubu Roi*. Who but Ubu could conclude a chapter recording these transactions with the reflection that the Secretariat 'must stand guard against the assaults which continue to be made against its international integrity and ideal'?

The manipulation of an oracle, a shrine or a holy place by a great prince or power for dynastic or national purpose is no new thing: the annals of both Delphi and the Vatican are rich in such matter. The vitality of the shrine, indeed, is demonstrated by its capacity to emerge from such experience, without altogether disgusting the faithful. The United Nations under Trygve Lie, then, must be thought of as having undergone, and survived, a test, as the Church survived the rule of so many mediocre and subservient pontiffs, both in Rome and at Avignon (and Mr Lie at least did not move the United Nations to Dallas, Texas). In fairness to this particular pontiff, it must be said that the trials of his pontificate were such that the throne, irrespective of the merits of its occupant at the time, must inevitably have been shaken.[23] Mr Lie forfeited the confidence of the Soviet Union, but if he had not done so—granted the circumstances of the Korean war—he would have been at the very least in grave danger of forfeiting that of the United States, and therefore of the majority in the Security Council and General Assembly. It is worth considering, however, how this very difficult situation might have been handled so as not to diminish and if possible to enhance, the charisma of the United Nations.

The first essential, it seems to me, was to stand on the plain meaning of the Charter; strained interpretations of Scripture strain also the faith of plain men, and weaken the authority of the Church. It is natural and to be expected that parties to a dispute will interpret the Charter to suit their case, and will find distinguished international lawyers to support their interpretation;

---

[22] *In the Cause of Peace*, p. 398.

[23] It must also be said that *before* the Korean crisis, Mr Lie had tried to preserve impartiality, and had consequently incurred a certain amount of displeasure from both sides. The United States had been displeased by his position on Iran (1946) and on the representation of China (early 1950). From June 1950 on however he became a militantly Western Secretary-General, even announcing in Norway in August 1950 his support for NATO. In an article, 'The United Nations and Trygve Lie' (Foreign Affairs, October 1950) the *New York Times* U.N. correspondent, Thomas Hamilton, notes that 'Some delegates . . . hint that Mr Lie's burst of activity in his final year in office was inspired at least in part by his desire for re-election'. The manner of his re-election did nothing to dispel this impression.

it is all the more incumbent on the Secretary-General to bow to what the Charter actually says—that is to say its meaning as apparent, or at least explicable, not so much to international lawyers as to 'us the peoples of the United Nations' who are supposed to have 'Resolved to Combine our Efforts to Accomplish these Aims' in the Charter. On this principle, the Secretary-General would have been absolutely right to raise the question of the North Korean attack, under Article 99 (which is what he claims he did) as a matter 'which in his [the Secretary-General's] opinion may threaten international peace and security'. To do so in no way compromised his office, or weakened his power to mediate. But when he interpreted Article 27 contrary to its plain meaning, and when he supported the 'Uniting for Peace' procedure—contrary to the sense of the Charter and to the known intent of its framers—then he did weaken the office. Whatever he said or did, the United States would have got their vote in the Security Council, in the absence of the Soviet Union, and—when 'vetoed' by the return of the Soviet delegation—in the Assembly; furthermore, even without these decisions they were determined to act anyway, as they showed by 'jumping the gun' on the Security Council's resolution of 27 June. Mr Lie mentions 'some quarters' which questioned his Korean stand: 'They said I should have attempted to mediate the war (thus allowing the aggressor to press his attack while I was talking to him and, quite possibly, to occupy all of Korea) rather than directing all my energies towards mobilising a United Nations army to throw back the aggressor.'[24]

It is very remarkable that the holder of the office of Secretary-General should have propagated such a misconception of the nature of the office, of the United Nations, and of reality generally. Mr Lie writes as if he had material power at his disposal, and neglects the moral power which was all he actually had. It was not in the Secretary-General's power to prevent the aggressor from occupying all (or any) of Korea, nor was he 'mobilising a United Nations army'; it was the United States which was fighting the war. If he had 'talked'—that is to say, if he had kept himself in a position to mediate—this would not have impeded or delayed the United States military operations; it might have given the Soviet Union an opportunity to save face and make peace.

In this vitally important crisis in the history of the United Nations, the holder of the office of Secretary-General, in grasping at an easy form of dramatic success, neglected the aspect of the sacred which alone gives meaning to the drama. The holder of the office, when he is true to its sacred function, must be

[24] *In the Cause of Peace*, p. 342.

touched by the spirit of the goddess Athena in the last scene of the *Oresteia:* neither abetting the Eumenides nor rebuking them, safeguarding the retreat of Orestes, applying the holy balm of noble words to all parties, and breaking the cycle of blood and vengeance. A Secretary-General acting on this level might have shortened the Korean war, by sanctifying a Communist retreat, through Soviet pressure on North Korea, accompanied by a solemn ritual of praise for Soviet 'mediation'. Mr Lie's successor might have attained this: the Aeschylean mode was within his reach. Mr Lie, however, all too obviously thought in terms not of Aeschylus but of an American scenario, of 'keeping the United Nations'—as he says himself—' "in the picture" '. As to the nature of 'the picture', Mr. Vyshinsky was perceptive:

'[Mr Lie] is to be commander-in-chief of the armed forces of the General Assembly . . . riding on a white horse. . . .'

The spectacle of Vyshinsky 'prosecuting' Trygve Lie is rich in poetic irony. Both of them had played their parts, more than a decade before, in the long process of the destruction of the great tragic hero of the century, Leon Trotsky. At that time also Mr Lie had the opportunity to play a part of classic magnaminity, and on that occasion also he muffed it. The play then was Sophocles' *Oedipus at Colonus*. Trotsky had sought asylum in Norway, where Trygve Lie was the Minister for Justice. The part assigned to Lie by destiny was that of King Theseus, welcoming the great exile and extending to him his protection. Lie welcomed, and failed to protect. As Isaac Deutscher relates in *The Prophet Outcast*, Lie personally welcomed Trotsky and even took from him an article for publication. Then Vyshinsky started baying for blood in Moscow, and Lie took fright, attempted to impose conditions on Trotsky which would have meant the cessation of his political work, accused him of violating conditions which Trotsky said he had never accepted, obtained from the King special decrees enabling him to place Trotsky under restraint, and finally deported him.

In *Oedipus at Colonus*, Theseus is the custodian of a shrine and it is in that capacity that he resists the pressures and plots directed by the Thebans against the inconvenient exile. As Minister for Justice of Norway, Lie was not the custodian of a shrine, but as Secretary-General of the United Nations he became just that. His original nomination as custodian required the consent of the Soviet authorities, who were of course well aware of his role in the harrying of the exile whom they had later murdered: Stalin still ruled. In agreeing to this nomination, therefore, they were agreeing that the guardian of the shrine should be a person who had in the past proved compliant.

There is poetic irony in the fact that when the stress became heavy, he did indeed prove compliant, not with them but with others whose authority in the region of the shrine and in relation to its guardian, was greater than theirs.

Pressures to degrade the shrine, by manipulating its drama for sectional advantage, are as old as civilisation; they are indeed part of the nature of the shrine and of its drama. But if they operate too crudely and too one-sidedly for too long the drama will lose its grip and the shrine its authority. The United Nations was in grave danger in this sense, at the end of Trygve Lie's tenure and as a result of his interpretation of his peace-keeping role in Korea.

9 BY HIS style, his sense of mission, his feeling for the sacred and for high drama, Dag Hammarskjold restored and enhanced the authority of the shrine and of its guardian. But on him too, and on the United Nations as restored by him, a 'peace-keeping role' brought disaster. I have already discussed the Congo crisis in so far as it relates to the subject of this essay. Here I should like to discuss the peace-keeping role of the Secretary-General, its limitations and dangers, as they appear after reflection on the lessons of the Congo.

A Secretary-General who accepts responsibility for a peace-keeping mission not only steps down from the religious level of politics, to the level of applied politics; he also, in reality though not in form, steps outside the service of the United Nations. He still serves the organisation, in theory, but in practice he serves an enterprise originally blessed by the United Nations: a very significant distinction. After the 'blessing' some States, not all and not even most, will actively join in the 'blessed' operation. In Korea, it was the United States and some of its allies; in the Congo it was African and Asian States plus two 'neutral' Europeans—friendly to the United States—all with the logistic, technical and financial backing of the United States and Canada; in some future operation (as in South-West Africa) it might conceivably be African and Asian States, with the logistic, financial and perhaps military backing of the Soviet Union. Each operation thus takes on a life and momentum of its own; it is an enterprise conducted in the name of the United Nations but *it is not in fact itself* the United Nations. It escapes almost immediately from the control of the Security Council, because of what I have described elsewhere as 'the ratchet mechanism'. That is to say that if those responsible for the operation appear—in the eyes of the Soviet Union—to have misinterpreted their instructions, their interpretation will almost certainly be upheld by the United States; and vice versa. As these are 'veto' situations the Council can never over-rule the interpretation of its actions. Re-legitimation, if required, is to be obtained from the General Assembly—that is to say from an American Afro-Asian consensus. If it is doubtful that re-legitimation can be obtained the supporters of the operation will continue under the authority of the old resolutions, as interpreted by the Secretary-General in consultation with the principal backers of the undertaking. The connection with 'the United Nations' becomes diffuse and amorphous.

Now the Secretary-General, if he must take responsibility for such an operation, loosely related as it is to the main organs, necessarily takes on a different persona. He is no longer just the servant of the major organs, under the Charter—the high priest

of the shrine. He becomes an embattled Prince-bishop in pursuit of objectives which, though sanctified by the shrine, are none the less practical and secular. It is vital for him to retain the support of the principal Power backing the operation, and that, so far—in all major operations—has meant the United States. He must also strive, though not with the same degree of urgency, to retain the confidence of the other States participating. Even at this stage—within the operation itself—he may come under heavy pressure to prevaricate, and eventually to lie. He may have to do so—as a national military commander does without scruple—if he is not to court failure in the operation assigned to him. For the policies of the principal Power involved, and of the participating States, are not necessarily identical; in the Congo the policies of the United States on the one hand and of, say, Ghana and India on the other, were not identical. Since the two sets of pressures are not equal, the Secretary-General is almost compelled to carry out, in essentials, the policy of the principal Power, dressed in the language most acceptable to the participating States.

The pressure to prevaricate, heavy within the operation itself, becomes almost compulsive when it is a question of explaining the operation to those Member governments who have remained outside it and are critical of it, as was the case, in relation to the Congo, with Britain, France and the Soviet Union. This pressure is likely to result in 'toned-down', disguised and in extreme instances, plainly false, reports of controversial events. One notable example of that is given in the chapter 'The Fire in the Garage' in my book, *To Katanga and Back*. But the matter has wider implications. 'Peace-keeping operations' requiring the use of force involve responsibility for the actions of soldiers, and the actions of soldiers, whether in combat conditions or not, are not going to be always such that the chief priest of peace can with any propriety carry responsibility for them. In my Katanga book I laid stress on the invention of 'U.N. atrocities' by the local Belgians and their friends. It is true that such incidents were invented and propagated on a great scale. But Irish officers, whose word I have no hesitation in accepting, have told me that this passage in my book is in part misleading. Most of the atrocity stories were indeed fabricated, but not all. They had good reason to believe that, on one occasion in September 1961, one contingent under United Nations command had killed Katangese paracommandos who had laid down their arms and sought to surrender. In the later, more extensive, hostilities there seem to have been further incidents of this kind.

Mr Tavares de Sá, in his chapter 'Publicity on the East River', cites the case of a colonel in the Indian brigade under U.N.

command who told the press (*Le Figaro*, Paris) that his men would take no prisoners; he tells also of the subsequent contortions and 'clarifications' designed to save the U.N.'s peace-loving face. In this context he refers, with implied disapproval, to 'disingenuous attitudes of U.N. officials in the Congo', but the fact was that the nature of a peace-keeping operation was such as to elicit 'disingenuous attitudes' not only in the Congo but also—and mainly—at Secretariat headquarters. In this case the 'U.N. official in the Congo' who sent a message which Mr de Sá describes as 'drafted with consummate skill in Secretariat bureaucratese; a minor masterpiece in ambiguity, hinting strongly that *Le Figaro*'s correspondent was lying, but without ever saying so unequivocally',[1] was doing exactly what U.N. headquarters expected of him: I would wager that he is not only still in U.N. service, but that he has been promoted. For a statement confirming that the colonel had said what he did say would have been exceedingly awkward. Some Western powers, who were well informed about the content of U.N. cables from the Congo—the technical personnel responsible for encoding and decoding these cables from the Congo were provided by a NATO power, and there were also other well-placed possible sources of information within the Secretariat—would have brought pressure to bear for the disciplining of the officer concerned. An attempt to have the officer disciplined after 'exposure' in the Western press would have been likely to mean trouble with India, the principal contributor of ground forces to the Congo operation: such an attempt might have led to the withdrawal of the Indian contingent, and a major set-back to the whole operation. So, from the point of view of the success of the operation, much the best solution was a report implying that what had been said had not been said. Officials at headquarters were then able with a clear conscience—or at any rate a conscience not additionally clouded—to inform the public that they had gone into the matter and that it appeared, from despatches received from the responsible civilian official, that the press reports were based on a misunderstanding. Later, in one's memoirs, it would be possible to deplore the 'disingenuous attitude' of the men on the spot, but at the time an 'ingenuous attitude'—like that of the colonel who said what he was doing instead of just doing it, out of sight of the press—would have been decidedly inconvenient. Officials in the Congo were never told that they were expected to lie in the cause of the success of the operation, but if they did not realise this immediately and intuitively, they would learn it eventually through trials and errors. For where force is, there must ruse also be.

[1] *The Play Within the Play*, p. 294.

10

No MAN, then, can carry a halo safely through a major peace-keeping operation. In most cases this does not matter; most people don't have haloes in the first place and don't need them. But the Secretary-General of the United Nations does need one, and we need him to have one; it is essential for his holy and mediating role in the sacred drama. The Secretary-General who assumes responsibility for a peace-keeping operation is leaving the sphere of the sacred for that of the temporal. There will be times when the peace-keeping operation goes smoothly, as did some of the temporal undertakings of the Popes. The United States Observation Group in the Lebanon for example did nothing to compromise the Secretary-General; rather it enhanced his standing and provided a 'precedent'—very important in Hammarskjold's eyes—for the Congo operation, strengthening for a time the disastrously false impression that it is in the interests of the United Nations, and of peace, to entrust such responsibilities to the Secretary-General.

The United States Expeditionary Force in the Middle East continued for years, as a responsibility of the Secretary-General, without compromising his authority. But when the crisis came, in 1967, the authority of the Secretary-General was inevitably compromised. By withdrawing the troops he incurred harsh and damaging criticism[1] in the West and in Israel: had he tried to keep them there, against the will of the Egyptian Government, he would have been denounced by the other camp. In either case the credibility of his mediating role—for this crisis and for others—was certain to be seriously impaired. The more important and delicate the operation, the more likely it is to compromise permanently the man responsible for it, in the eyes of at least some Member governments, and of the wider public. Thus the damage which responsibility for major operations is likely to do to the Secretary-General's effectiveness far outweighs the increases in prestige coming from the success of minor enterprises. The Secretary-General who has been directly involved in a temporal adventure returns to the sacred drama with a tarnished persona. His moral stature will have been impaired by propaganda and innuendo and sometimes also by bloodshed and the lies which precede and follow it; his dignity will have suffered by his involvement in something very much resembling a scuffle. The Goddess Athena must not be seen kicking the Eumenides on the shins or feigning ignorance of the whereabouts of Orestes. As the man responsible for a major peace-keeping operation may be forced to perform the equivalents

[1] A well-known *New York Times* commentator publicly described U Thant as having acted in this matter 'with the dynamism of a noodle', a comment neither justified by the facts nor calculated to increase respect for the office of Secretary-General.

of these actions, he can no longer, when he returns to the stage, properly play the part of the Goddess Athena. And this is the part which he must be able to play, for which he must hold himself in reserve, for which he must remain ritually pure.

The height of sacred authority which Hammarskjold had attained, by the beginning of the Congo operation, is recorded by Mr Tavares de Sá, an eye-witness not unduly predisposed to veneration. He tells of Hammarskjold's address to the Security Council on 20 July, 1960, reporting that 'the U.N. has embarked on its single, biggest effort under U.N. colours, organised and directed by the U.N. "itself" ' [thereby marking off this operation from that which had undone his predecessors]. Hammarskjold went on to remind Member states of their responsibilities: 'because we are at a turn of the road where our attitudes will be of decisive significance, I believe, not only for the future of the Organisation but also for the future of Africa. And Africa may well in the present circumstances mean the world.'

Mr Tavares de Sá records the response of the audience, or congregation:

'Today it is hard to evoke with any credibility the reception given to these last words, delivered with that restrained, almost metallic tone that Hammarskjold reserved for his more dramatic pronouncements and which was a refined form of theatricality. His words were received in the galleries by a reverent, awed silence more appropriate for a cathedral than for the Council chamber.'[2]

The riot in these same galleries less than seven months later is symbolic of the breaking of a spell. Not that Hammarskjold ever lacked loyal or even fanatical admirers—hundreds of thousands in the West and some elsewhere were soon to mourn him as a martyr—but that he had become the symbol of a party within the United Nations, and no longer of the United Nations itself. He was a man to be cheered or hooted, no longer one to be heard in 'reverent awed silence'. He had incurred the open hostility of one permanent member, the guarded opposition of two others, and the all too enthusiastic support of a fourth (the fifth, 'China', has no autonomous significance). Even in those countries most friendly to him, the public was at best puzzled by the continuing 'mess in the Congo' and the United Nations' strange alternations between 'powerlessness' and strong action. The continued use of the style and language appropriate to his sacred persona, while referring to the profane activities in the Congo placed a further strain on the office. He was drawing very heavily both on the credit of his office and on his personal credit when he used the following language to the General Assembly on 26 September, 1960:

[2] *The Play Within the Play*, p. 269.

'Time and again the United Nations has had to face situations in which a wrong move might have tended to throw the weight of the Organisation over in favour of this or that specific party in a conflict of a primarily domestic character. To permit that to happen is indeed to intervene in domestic affairs contrary to the letter and the spirit of the Charter.'

Those—few, but important—who knew what had happened in Leopoldville a few weeks before those words were spoken could not, even if they approved of what had been done, have the same kind of respect for the speaker as they had had before. If they respected him still—and he was a man to command personal respect, even from his enemies, in the worst of circumstances—it was not as a holy man but as a wily one: the resourceful, ruthless captain of a tricky enterprise. When a Secretary-General comes to attract that kind of admiration he can no longer adequately discharge his sacred function.

In all this, of course, there was a deep personal tragedy in that the Secretary-General who was forced by circumstances to lower the office from the holy to the wily, was probably of all important public men of his time the most disposed to holiness. He was also the only Secretary-General known to have had a conviction of the sacred character of his own role (as *Markings* reveals). Similarly, of course, certain of the Popes exalted and magnified the sacred character of their office, and at the same time were led to profane it by the unedifying methods necessary to sustain their temporal projects.

Just how grave the implications of such a profanation are for the United Nations we can see immediately if we consider that crisis which brought the world nearest to the brink of thermo-nuclear war: the Cuban missile crisis of October, 1962. If Hammarskjold had still been alive, and Secretary-General, he could have played no part in the resolution of that crisis, since he was regarded by one of the powers in confrontation as being a tool of the other. Thant—who had the Congo operation thrust on him, and who had not been responsible for the key decisions —did not suffer from the same disability. He was able, therefore, to make an appeal which the Soviet Union could heed with propriety if it wished to do so, as it did. Mr de Sá makes some valid comments on the Soviet decision to turn back the ships:

'. . . It was apparent to the whole world that they were submitting to American power; at that juncture the U.N. gave Moscow a way to save face. The ships were diverted because the Secretary-General of the United Nations had asked comrade Premier Khrushchev to consider the interest of world peace— not the threat of U.S. destroyers.

'Of course the U.N. provided only a face-saving device, but

IN SESSION
WINTER 1966

December 8, 1966
Security Council on Rhodesia

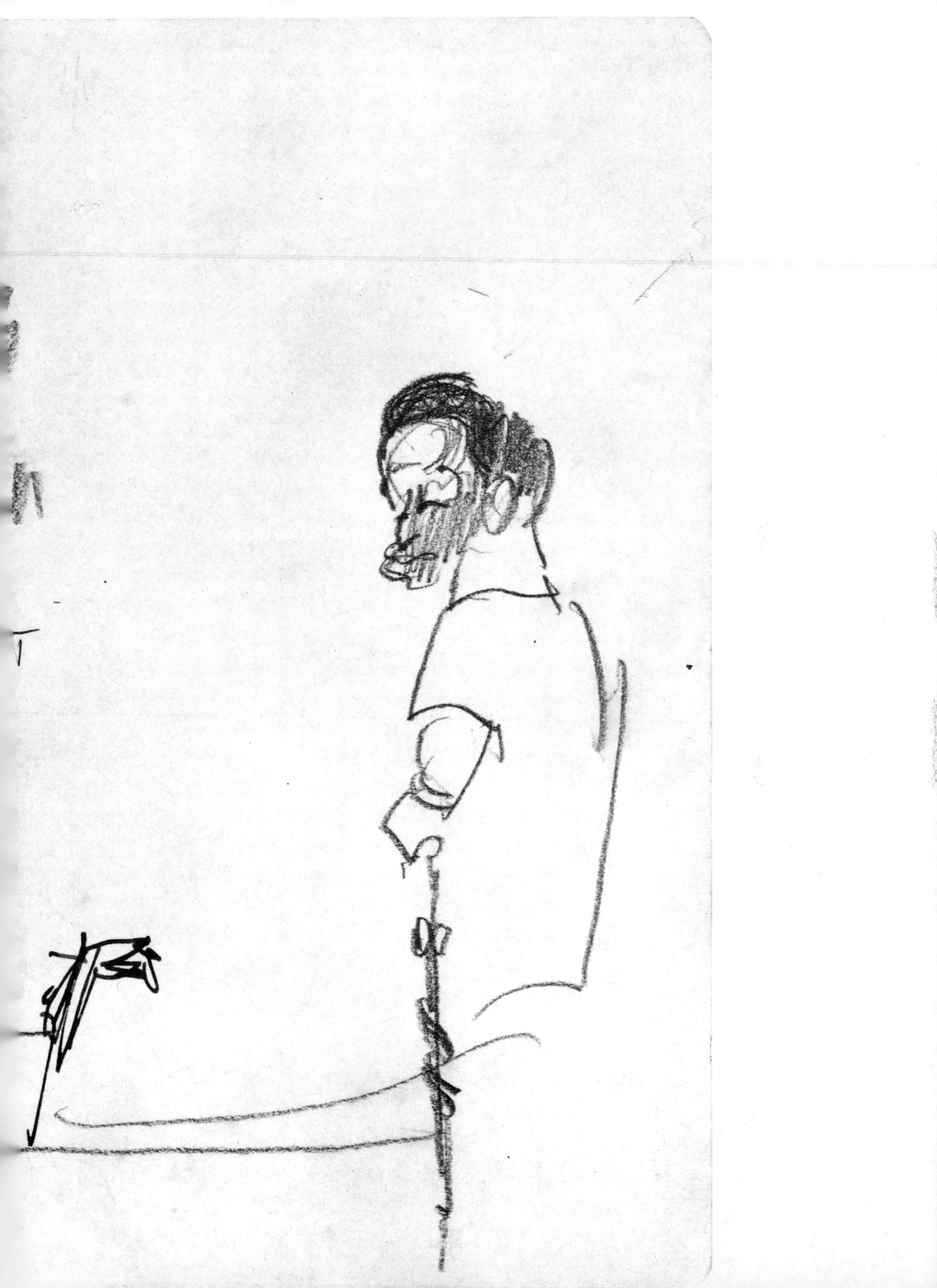

Sixth Committee 954th Meeting
10.12.66 Trusteeship Council Chamber
Technical assistance to promote the teaching,
study, dissemination and wider appreciation
of international law:
Report of the Secretary-General
(A/6422 and Add.1; A/C.6/L.611/
Rev.1 and Add 1-2) [86]

12-12-66 Security Council: Senegal delegate speaks

MALI

12.12.1966 UN Security Council on Rhodesia

1333rd Meeting of the Security Council UN 12.12.1966

U Thant   Dr Ralph J. Bunche

13.12.66 Security Council 1335th meeting

ENGLISH 2 | FRENCH 3 | RUSSIAN | SPANISH | CHINESE

Sheikh Suleiman bin Himyar, King of the Green Mountain

Talib bin Ali (brother of the Imam Ghalib bin Ali)

16.12.1966 UN Security Council 1338th meeting

North Delegates Lounge

20.12.66 15h00
General Assembly
Closing Speech

YES 1 799 6
NO 0 0
ABSTAIN 1 4

COLOMBIA
ISRAEL

Lounge

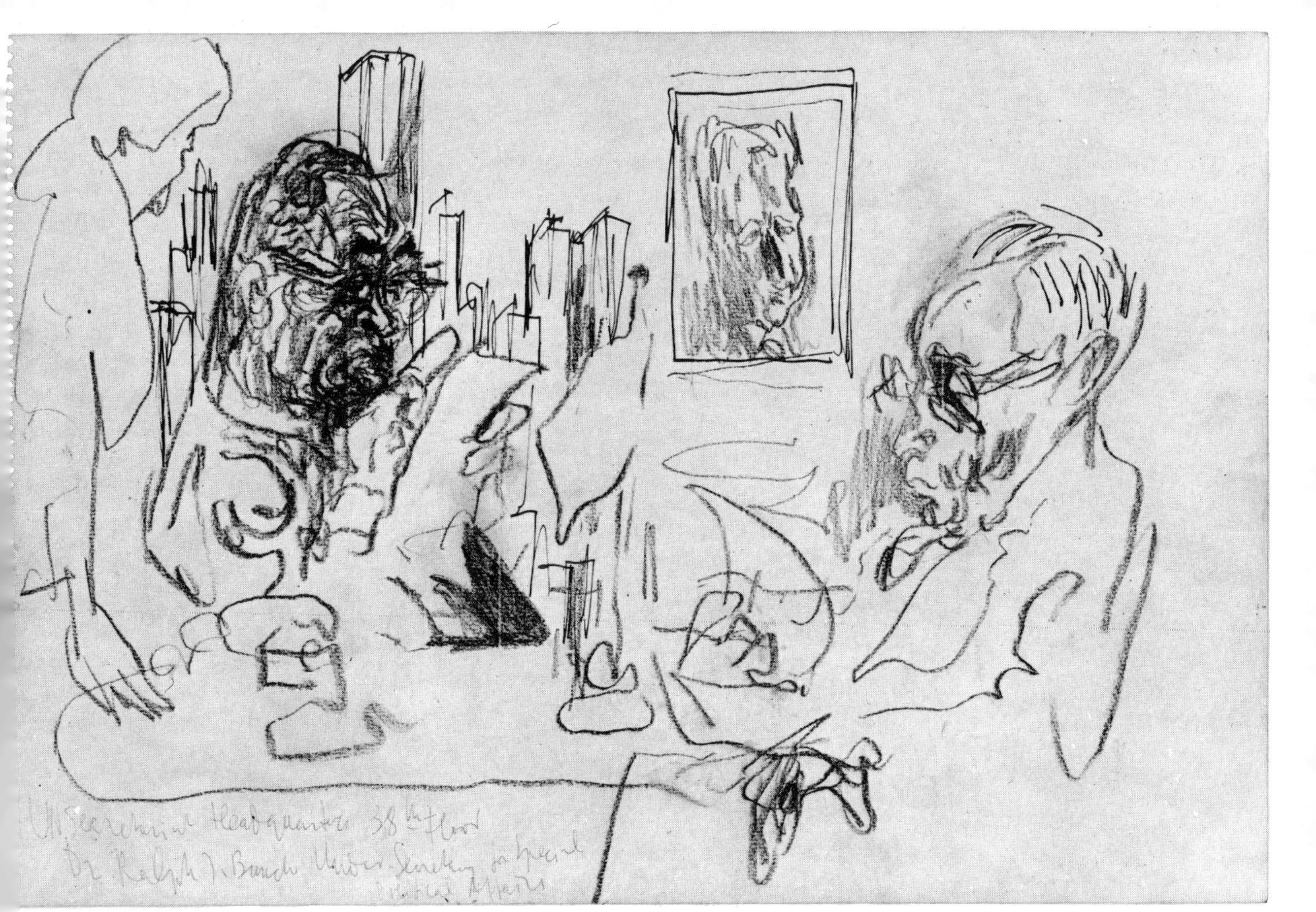
UN Secretariat Headquarters 38th Floor
Dr Ralph J. Bunche Under-Secretary for Special Political Affairs

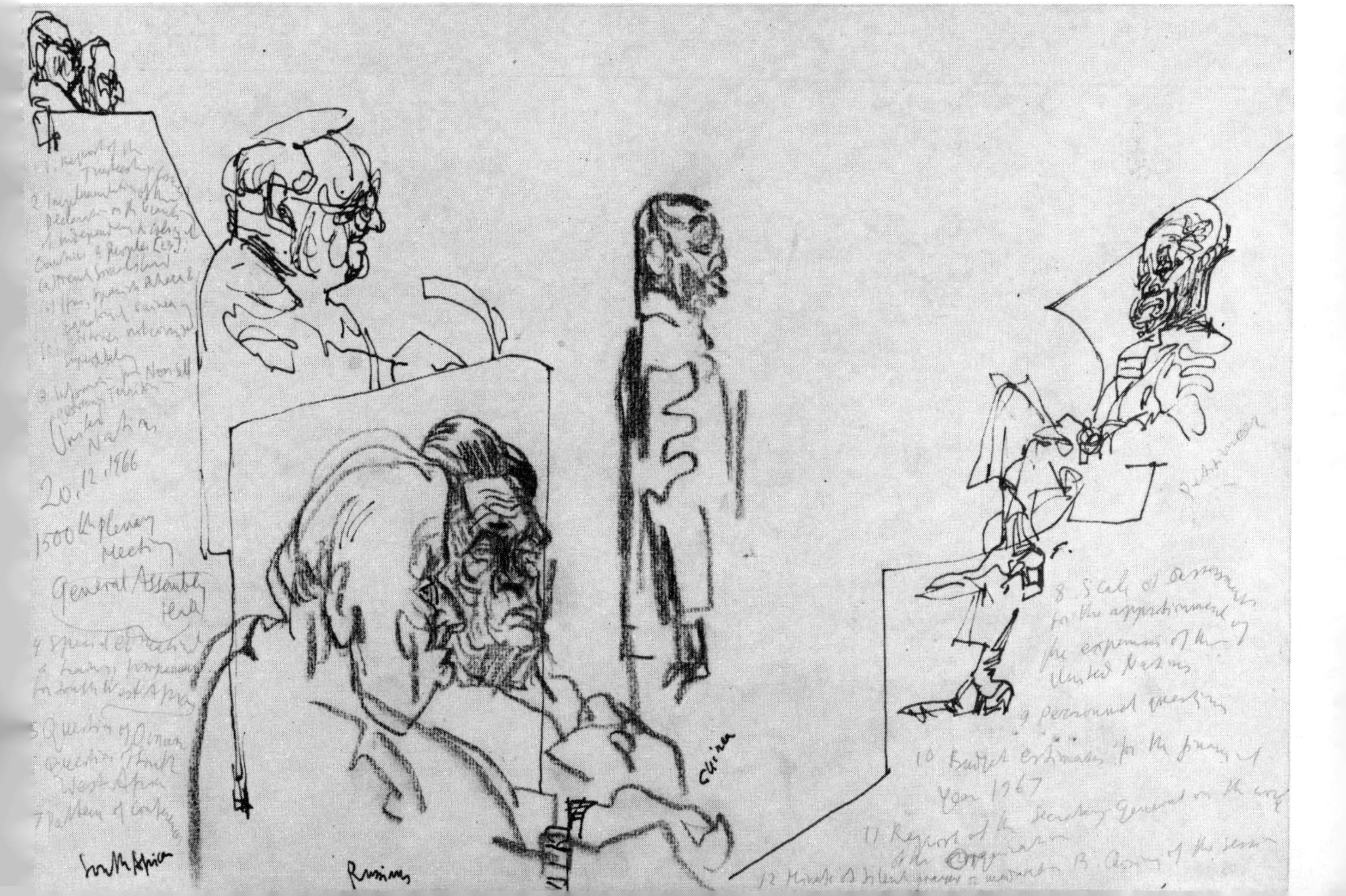
United Nations
20.12.1966
1500th Plenary Meeting
General Assembly Hall
8 Scale of assessments for the apportionment of the expenses of the United Nations
9 Personnel questions
10 Budget estimates for the financial year 1967
11 Report of the Secretary-General on the work of the Organization
China
Russians
South Africa

Delegates' Lounge

this should not be lightly dismissed. In a political-military crisis of the first magnitude a great power may find itself forced to court even the danger of nuclear war if the alternative is an intolerable and widely-publicised loss of prestige.'[3]

It is apparent, therefore, that if the rites are not so conducted as to conserve the maximum charisma for the sacred drama and for its central figure, the Secretary-General, then the emergency performance, which may be the last barrier between humanity and self-destruction, may be prevented from exercising its saving power.

From these considerations there derives logically the following proposition:

The involvement of the Secretary-General in a local, peace-keeping operation increases the danger of world war.

This is, of course, not the same as saying that the United Nations must keep out of local peace-keeping operations. It cannot do so, if only because agreement to have such operations carried out—that is to provide the blessing and insignia for their execution—may be the outcome of a major success in international mediation. The otherwise pointless United Nations Expeditionary Force in Egypt had to go there to pretend to carry out the peace-keeping task which Britain and France had pretended to assume there. These powers could no longer sustain the fiction ('separating the combatants)' under cover of which they had invaded Egypt. Drama being kin to fiction, it was entirely appropriate that the General Assembly should come to the rescue of this shade, and save the honour of Britain and France, by asking other members to act out, in co-operation with Egypt and in restraint of Israel, the fulfilment of the nominal task which, in the hands of Britain and France; had involved invading Egypt in collusion with Israel. By this apostolic succession of pious fictions the peace was preserved, and the 'combatants', at last, really separated.[4] This is an area in which scepticism on the part of the general public would be fatal, and in which a willing suspicion of disbelief is as appropriate as for other forms of drama, and more necessary. But the point here is that the face-saving agon, which is an essential part of preserving world peace in critical circumstances, may lead to the actual assumption of responsibility for armed expeditions, which may, if things go badly, as they sometimes will, compromise the role of the Secretary-General in the next agon.

---

[3] *The Play Within the Play*, p. 276.

[4] Until, more than ten years later, President Nasser rejected the remains of the fiction which had protected him—and felt the blast of reality.

11

THE PROBLEM then is essentially this: how to preserve the spiritual authority of the Secretary-General, which must sometimes be used to invoke a blessing on local peace-keeping operations, from being contaminated and perhaps effaced by contact with the temporal conduct of such operations?

The problem is not resolved by the fact of having a Military Commander, because in operations organised and directed by personnel appointed by the United Nations itself (which means all U.N. operations so far except Korea) the over-riding considerations are diplomatic and political, and the Commander is in practice a high military adviser to the civilians who must take the political decisions, with an eye on the diplomatic conjuncture, and an ear to the American Embassy. He can remonstrate—and threaten resignation—but in the last resort it is the civilians who decide. General von Horn, former U.N. Commander in the Congo, records that on one occasion when he refused to issue a certain directive to the troops under his command, the senior civilian official on the spot simply bypassed him, transmitting the directive in question himself to unit commanders.[1] General von Horn was a weak Commander, and it is hard to imagine either General Alexander or General MacEoin submitting to being bypassed in this way; the principle of civilian control is, however, firmly established. In such an operation as that in the Congo those in charge are working under the spiritual authority of ambiguous and sometimes contradictory resolutions of the Security Council and/or Assembly. Someone must interpret these documents, not only in the light of their actual wording, and of the Charter, but also of the interpretations known to be assigned to them by the principal Powers concerned, and of both the *real* attitudes, intentions and capacities of these powers, and their *dramatic* positions which, having been acted out in the Council or the Assembly, have also a certain limited influence over their actual behaviour. This task of interpretation, with its multiple variables, is obviously one, not for a soldier, but for a civilian highly experienced in international affairs—and even he will court disaster at every turn, and eventually encounter almost certain disaster, in a major operation, as there accumulate behind him the broken remains of interpretations cherished by various Powers and necessarily at some point rejected by him. Nor is the problem resolved by having a Special Representative or Officer-in-Charge on the spot or spots, as long as that officer reports to the Secretary-General, as in the Congo. Normally the officer-in-charge will be acting under the directives of the Secretary-General, who will 'interpret' the resolutions for him in ticklish cases, but even when the

[1] *Soldiering for Peace*, pp. 185–7.

Special Representative acts without instructions the Secretary-General is likely to be forced to accept responsibility. Thus at the decisive moment when Andrew Cordier—then the senior U.N. representative in the Congo—moved against Patrice Lumumba, Hammarskjold accepted responsibility for actions about which he apparently was not consulted in advance. As he told the Security Council at its meeting on 9–10 September:

'The two far-reaching steps of an emergency nature (closing the radio and airports) which were taken by the U.N. representatives . . . were not preceded by any reference of the matter to me, because of the extreme urgency of the problem our people were facing on the spot . . . I was not consulted but I fully endorse the action taken.'

If Hammarskjold had repudiated Cordier's action he would have lost the confidence of the United States: as he endorsed the action, he lost that of the Soviet Union. Whatever choice he made, his usefulness as a mediator was certain to be damaged beyond repair. His spiritual authority was also damaged by the necessity to prevaricate. He could not present the only adequate justification of what the United Nations representative had actually done: the argument that it was necessary, on the same grounds as those for which the United Nations had originally gone in—that is to prevent another 'Spain', in which the rival factions would invite in contending powers. To prevent a 'Spain', the United Nations had accepted Lumumba's invitation to the Congo; still to prevent a 'Spain' they had brought down Lumumba once he started to 'bring in the Russians', (i.e. to accept Russian logistic aid for the Central Government's campaign against the secessionist regimes in South Kasai and Katanga) thereby evoking the danger of a Russo-American confrontation in the heart of Africa. It is not a negligible argument, but Hammarskjold was debarred from using it, since nothing would more quickly have lost him African support than an admission that the United Nations had helped to overthrow an African Prime Minister. He accordingly described the U.N. role in the Congo as 'a role of utter discretion and impartiality'. It was not, and it was not possible that it should be. On the very day that Hammarskjold spoke in this vein, Colonel Mobutu received 5,000,000 francs from the United Nations[2] and four days later he neutralised Lumumba (and Kasavubu too, no doubt to prove discretion and impartiality) and expelled the Soviet Embassy.

Hammarskjold himself made some attempt to resolve the spiritual-temporal dilemma by assuming two aspects: that of the Secretary-General in his essence, and that of the Secretary-

---

[2] Hoskyns, *The Congo Since Independence*, p. 231, and n. 29.

General under the accidents—in both the theological and ordinary senses—of his responsibility, for the United Nations Operation in the Congo. Thus when he made his fatal decision to fly to Ndola to meet Tshombe, and I asked permission to join his flight at Kamina, I was told that he intended to handle the discussions 'outside the framework of ONUC' (*Opération des Nations Unies au Congo*); clearly he did not want his spiritual authority to be contaminated by our all too temporal activities in Katanga. This distinction—to which the present writer probably owes his life—was, however, too fine to be generally useful. In the eyes of the world he continued to carry, in all his activities, his Congo responsibilities—responsibilities for his own past actions, and Cordier's and Khiary's and mine, and for the versions of those actions which he had promulgated to the world. In so far as he was compromised, the office of the Secretary-General was compromised too, and the world's margin of safety in emergencies significantly reduced.

The problem cannot be safely resolved unless the spiritual and temporal roles can be sharply separated, and the Secretary-General confined to the spiritual role. This would not require revision of the Charter; all it would require is that the permanent members of the Security Council, and their friends and satellites in the Assembly, and the leading African and Asian countries should realise their common, vital interest in preserving the spiritual authority of the Secretary-General, and realise also the danger, now clearly established, which the use of temporal power —in peace-keeping operations—implies for the spiritual authority.

If this is realised, it is quite possible, under the Charter, to protect the Secretary-General from responsibility for the execution of peace-keeping operations. Indeed, keeping him out of such operations is more 'Charter-like' than bringing him in. The only specific function conferred on the Secretary-General by the Charter in this area is that he 'may bring to the attention of the Security Council any matter which in his opinion may threaten the maintenance of international peace and security' (Article 99). Chapter VII of the Charter—'Action with Respect to Threats to the Peace, Breaches of the Peace, and Acts of Aggression'—makes no mention at all of the Secretary-General. The 'temporal' peace-keeping functions which have been conferred on him are presumably in virtue of Article 97, which designates the Secretary-General as 'the Chief administrative officer of the Organisation', and Article 98, which says that in that capacity he 'shall perform such functions as are entrusted to him by [the General Assembly, the Security Council, etc.]'. There is nothing in all this which requires that it should be the Secretary-General personally who undertakes responsibility for a given peace-keeping operation. The present writer is not alone in thinking that it is dangerous to ask the Secretary-General to carry such responsibility. Mr Peter Calvocoressi, for example, approaching the problem on the basis of assumptions rather different from mine, writes as follows.

'In theory the Security Council or General Assembly tells the Secretary-General what to do. In practice these instructions are too vague or general to be applied without further interpretation. This interpretation has in the past fallen to the Secretary-General who was in effect required to fill a gap between resolution and action. Such a burden on one man is too great and endangers the whole system of collective responsibility by off-loading too much of the responsibility from the collective to an individual. In the Congo for instance the Secretary-General was authorised to use force, but in circumstances and for purposes that were inadequately defined. Some means must be devised —perhaps an extension of the Advisory Committee—to spread the responsibility without derogating from the Secretary-General's permanent position within the Secretariat.'[3]

It is not, in the present writer's opinion, so much a matter of 'spreading' the responsibility as of keeping it away from the Secretary-General. The Advisory Committee on the Congo was (as I know from direct experience in 1960–61) a harmless body which was invited to approve the Secretariat's version of events which had already taken place, and to endorse general and impeccable propositions about future policies. It did nothing to relieve the Secretary-General of responsibility, and it is doubtful if any Committee could effectively carry executive responsibility for a peace-keeping operation. What is required is that there shall be an executive officer, *other than the Secretary-General*, who shall carry responsibility—with or without the advice of a Committee or Committees—for peace-keeping operations. It would be quite possible for either the Security Council or the General Assembly, when legitimising a peace-keeping operation, to request the Secretary-General to nominate, say, a *Co-ordinator*, who would assist in combining the efforts of those member nations engaging in the operation in question or supporting it, and report directly to the principal organs on the progress of the operation which they had legitimised. The Co-ordinator could draw on the resources of the Secretariat, by arrangement with the Secretary-General, but the Secretary-General would not carry responsibility for his operations.

Such arrangements would protect the sanctity of the Secretary-General, and his function as mediator. They would preserve the focus of cohesion within the sacred drama, since the

[3] *World Order and New States: Problems of Keeping the Peace* (1962), pp. 92–3.

Secretary-General's relation to the principal members would in no case be severed by the results of temporal responsibilities. Finally they would make more clear the religious character of the United Nations itself, as an entity having the authority to legitimise certain actions, and to review their continuing legitimacy, but not possessed of material power of its own to enforce decisions. This last distinction, which is of fundamental importance to the Organisation in the shape which it has actually taken,[4] has been blurred by the intrusion of the temporal, in the form of the Secretary-General's occasional role as *ad hoc* commander over armed men. Liberation from temporal responsibility would also allow the Secretary-General more time, free from day to day pressures, for thought and discussion directed towards the lowering of international tensions, and for the establishment of relations ready to stand the strain of an emergency. He would have much less to do, and he should have much less to do, and more time to think and, in a secular but sacred way, to pray.

It is true that the Co-ordinator, when things went seriously wrong, would be liable to become a scapegoat. That indeed is the central idea behind the proposal: the scapegoat is an ancient and necessary figure in ritual drama. The United Nations, or rather the Secretariat, has shown some instinctive appreciation of this: as one phase or another of the Congo operation 'went wrong'—that is to say attracted an unacceptable amount of reprobation from some important State or group of States—the usefulness of this or that official would be deemed to have become exhausted; this is the modern liturgic form of the ancient ceremony. But these sacrifices, sound as was the intention behind them, failed to appease, because the Secretary-General himself had held responsibility for the actions of the exhausted in the days of their usefulness. It was therefore unavailing to loose them into the wilderness, because an odour of undischarged goatishness continued to cling to the office of the Secretary-General; the temple itself became unclean. The role of a Co-ordinator (reporting direct to the Security Council and General Assembly) would mean that the office of the Secretary-General would at all times be preserved from contamination, and that—if things went seriously wrong—the act of purification, the scaping of the useful but exhausted goat, would be duly performed, complete and decisive. The Security Council cannot be contaminated because, if anything 'goes wrong' under its decisions this is because—in the opinion of the protesting party—its decisions have been misinterpreted. The 'Co-ordinator' procedure would allow for the departure of the misinterpreter, without compromising the office of the Secretary-General, or paralysing his mediatory function.

[4] Since the Military Staff Committee proved an impracticable aspiration.

12

THE DISENGAGEMENT of the Secretary-General from his temporal role in local peace-keeping is not, however, likely to be accomplished easily or quickly. The difficulty is not in finding people for the 'doom-shaped'—Thurber's word—office of Co-ordinator. There is never any lack of recruits for what are known as 'challenging' tasks. The real difficulty is in the nature of the sacred drama itself, and in the dramatic involvement of the characters. The participants in the drama, as well as the spectators, must take it seriously—and seriously, for most people, means literally. Most 'good United Nations people' will be likely to take umbrage—at first at least—at the theme of this book, because they are likely to feel that 'play-acting' is frivolous and trivial, and that the suggestion that they are 'play-acting' is therefore offensive and perhaps malicious. They are international statesmen, or international civil servants, and the suggestion that essentially they are mummers, even holy mummers acting out a great human ritual, will be frostily, perhaps contemptuously, received. For an effective rite, in contemporary terms, cannot be presented as a rite. Thurman Arnold, in *The Folklore of Capitalism*, showed how much there was of myth and ritual in systems that we habitually think of as sternly prosaic and practical, like corporation law. These myths and rituals, to be effective, must be thought of as pragmatic parts of an adult, advanced, scientific system. Now the United Nations—in which the elements of myth and ritual are much more pervasive, and those of material practicality much less so, than is the case with the legal and economic institutions described by Thurman Arnold—has all the more cause to stress its 'seriousness', that is to say to validate its myth by clothing it in the language of secular and material power. It has its 'executive' and 'legislative' organs and its 'civil service', just like a modern national government, in form and appearance. Round these shadowy organisms, just as round real, national ones (which of course also include elements of fantasy) there cluster pride, ambition, jealousy and esprit-de-corps. Within the Secretariat, the famous 'Indian chain of command' pursues its phantom peace-dance, in deadly earnest, as all good players must be. In the Assembly, the Committees sit late, amid at least as much tension, manœuvring and acrimony as could be the case if their 'legislation' had actual force of law. And the Security Council (or part of it) according its blessing to America's decision to intervene in Korea, performed as solemnly as if it were actually taking that decision itself.

Within this system, taken thus literally, the Secretary-General is not, of course, the priest of a shrine. He is 'the chief administrative officer of the Organisation'. As such he is at the head of a hierarchy indeed, but only, it is felt, in the dead-metaphor sense of an administrative hierarchy, a stratification of civil servants. He sits at the top of a glass palace, but it is a *modern* glass palace, a huge office-building on whose shining floors a multitude of more or less highly-paid officials are understood to be engaged in complex administrative tasks. In such a building the administrative illusion becomes pervasive, often in its purest and most intoxicating form, that of the administrator with nothing to administer. Now in the logic of the administrative illusion, the Secretary-General, being the 'chief administrative officer of the Organisation' *must not be bypassed*. Within this sub-system too, there is magic, taboo, the danger of contagion if the taboo is infringed. If the *chief administrative officer* should suffer the equivalent of ritual defilement within the administrative sub-cult—and that is what it means to be bypassed—then the whole administrative order is contaminated, and its function placed in doubt: 'If there is no God, how can I be a captain?'

Now the Secretary-General, by his day to day functions as 'chief administrative officer', is likely himself to be affected by the values of the sub-cult. In so far as he is so affected, he will wish to retain ultimate administrative control over all matters of importance within the purview of the United Nations, including peace-keeping operations. Members of the Security Council and General Assembly are likely also to wish to assign a function which they must regard as of importance—since otherwise they would not create it—to their *chief* functionary. There is nothing unacceptable about the idea of a Co-ordinator, in itself, but the idea of a Co-ordinator reporting *direct* to Security Council or Assembly, is likely to be repugnant to people who are acting the part of a civil service, or that of a government or parliament.

But a Co-ordinator reporting to the 'chief administrative officer', according to the commandments of the administrative religion, can do nothing to relieve the Secretary-General of those executive responsibilities, which, in the event of serious dissension about the conduct of the operation, may paralyse his mediatory functions, which infinitely transcend his administrative ones in importance, in terms of the purpose for which the United Nations was set up, as distinct from the metaphorical terms in which that purpose is clothed.

Administrative momentum, far from being slowed down, has actually been increased by the 'peace-keeping' operations, with their precious fuel of 'precedents'. Thus, when the United Nations became drawn into peace-keeping in Cyprus in 1964, the Secretary-General, instead of being 'insulated' was invited to send, and did send, his 'personal representative' to report back to him. As regards the armed forces, the Secretary-General told the Security Council on 2 March 1964 'that he intended in accordance with established practice concerning previous United Nations peace-keeping forces, to keep the Council promptly and fully informed about the organisation and operation of the force'. There is something eerie in the thought that the accumulated improvisations of the Congo operation—or the official versions of these improvisations—are now preserved for ever in a body of 'established practice'. Indeed there may well be two bodies of established practice: one, that of the past series of 'official versions' for use of the Security Council and General Assembly; the other, that of past actions as known to the Secretariat and used for its guidance. Combining the two, one imagines the following despatch:

'In accordance with established practice A (Secretariat), the Secretary-General's representative today financed a coup d'état, causing the overthrow of the Prime Minister and the expulsion of the Soviet Embassy. In accordance with established practice B (Secco and General Assembly) the Secretary-General kept the principal organs promptly and fully informed of the absolute discretion and impartiality with which his representatives were acting.'

In practice the Cyprus involvement has fortunately not so far compromised the Secretary-General or his office; the fact that it is a dispute among NATO members, rather than in an 'open area' of the Cold War, has probably operated to reduce its destructive potential. But what is ominous is the setting-in of administrative rigour: the assumption that 'the way it was done before'—even though it led to the paralysis of the mediating functions of a Secretary-General—is the way in which it must be done for ever. Some members of the Security Council had doubts: France thought that the Council was 'going very far in the direction of the delegation of powers to a single individual'; Czechoslovakia 'had serious doubts about giving the Secretary-General responsibilities which should, under the Charter, be part of the Security Council's functions'. These, with the USSR, abstained and the required resolution went through, worded in such a way as to embroil the Secretary-General as thoroughly as possible in the middle of any dispute that might arise between the Powers over Cyprus: . . . 'The composition and size of the Force shall be established by the Secretary-General in consultation with the governments of . . . The Commander of the Force shall be appointed by the Secretary-General and report to him. The Secretary-General, who shall keep the Governments providing the Force fully informed, shall report periodically to the Security Council on its operation . . . Recommends . . . that the Secretary-General designate . . . a mediator (who) shall report periodically to the Secretary-General on his efforts.'

If this kind of wording, closely binding the Secretary-General's office to the fluctuating fortunes of each peace-keeping mission, is now indeed 'established practice' then the office is placed in permanent jeopardy, and the effectiveness of the world's mediator exposed to the hazards of a thousand local incidents. It is a high price to pay for conventional ideas of administrative propriety.

Thus the metaphor of Organisation (with 'parliament', 'government' and 'civil service') which is necessary for the enactment of the sacred drama in a secular age, itself affects the performance of the drama and can endanger the fulfilment of its central purpose.

The dilemma of the necessary danger, the literalness which is inseparable from a live faith, and which yet may destroy the faith, is far older than the United Nations, and inherently beyond the reach of remedy. This is not to say, however, that the specific danger which executive responsibilities entail for the Secretary-General's mediatory function may not yet appear in so bright a light as to attract the attention even of worshippers in the administrative sub-cult. The fates of Lie and Hammarskjold, the paralysis of the Secretary-General's mediatory function during two and a half years of Lie's tenure (June 1950–November 1952) and one year of Hammarskjold's (September 1960–September 1961) form, after all, a conspicuous and disturbing pattern, though not, apparently, sufficiently so to have yet succeeded in shaking the devotees of established practice. During more than one-sixth of the United Nations' first twenty years, the office of the Secretary-General was incapacitated in respect of its essential function, because the Secretary-General was on speaking terms with only one of the two principal potential belligerents. Neither 'quiet diplomacy'—on whose importance both Lie and Hammarskjold laid so much stress—nor the reserve power of dramatic supplication in an emergency was possible under such conditions. The world's margin of safety was correspondingly diminished during these years.

For this situation the Soviet Union blamed Lie and Hammarskjold personally and the United States for manipulating them. Western opinion blamed the Soviet Union, accusing it of a desire 'to wreck the United Nations'. The personal factor cannot altogether be left out of account: it was Lie's zeal for getting 'the United Nations'—meaning himself—'into the picture', rather than any strong desire of the Security Council (minus one permanent member) or even of the United States to confer on the Secretary-General any responsibility for the conduct of the 'peace-keeping operation', that led to his ostracism by the Soviet Union, and this was prolonged and exacerbated by his clinging to office (after 1950) in a manner which the Soviet

Union was bound to consider illegal. In the second case, however, the principal operative factor was *not* the personality of the Secretary-General. It was the decision of the Security Council (including both the United States and the Soviet Union) on 14 July 1960 'to authorise the Secretary-General to take the necessary steps . . . to provide the (Government of the Congo) with such military assistance as may be necessary'—followed by its decision on 9 August 1960 to request him 'to continue to carry out the responsibility placed on him . . .' by the July resolution. The Soviet Union in voting in favour of both these resolutions, helped to impose on the Secretary-General a responsibility which could not be adequately discharged except by retaining the confidence of the United States, in conditions in which that could not be retained without losing the confidence of the Soviet Union. Hammarskjold made 'mistakes', but they were the mistakes of a man in a trap, in which any move, or abstention from moving, will turn out to be a mistake.

As for the Soviet Union, it is entirely unreasonable to blame it for its attacks on these Secretaries-General, or for breaking off relations with them. If any Secretary-General had used his office to an equivalent extent against the United States—as might theoretically have been done over the Bay of Pigs, the invasion of Santo Domingo, or the military intervention in Vietnam—the United States would most certainly have made his continued tenure impossible. (Imagine the fate of a Secretary-General who should take it on himself to subsidise say, a Santo Domingo colonel, who then immediately expelled the United States Embassy.) Nor is it reasonable to accuse the Soviet Union of seeking 'to wreck the United Nations'; the Soviet Union could at any time wreck the United Nations if it really wanted to do so, by simply walking out; without the second superpower, the other potential belligerent in world war, the sacred drama would lose all significance: for this part there can be no understudy.

13

THE 'BLAME-LAYING' interpretations of the past can now be laid to rest. The problem of the avoidance of such situations in the future is the problem of how to insulate the Secretary-General from such temporal responsibilities. If past experience has not sufficed to teach this lesson—and the terms of the Security Council's resolution of 4 March, 1964, on Cyprus suggest that it has not—then the shadow of a possible future may teach it. In an earlier section I showed that it is now within the bounds of possibility that a 'peace-keeping operation', *not desired by the United States*, might conceivably in certain conditions (some of which are already satisfied in relation to South-West Africa) be legitimised by a two-thirds vote in the General Assembly, in a rite previously recognised as valid by the United States. It would then be open to the Soviet Union—as in the past to the United States—to provide the material means for the execution of the legitimised operation. We may surmise that the United States would have doubts about the wisdom and propriety of associating the Secretary-General with such an enterprise. The mere existence of even the remote possibility of a *Soviet* action under 'Uniting for Peace' procedures would shed a new light on past experience, and help to render the United States and others more cautious about involving the Secretary-General in temporal affairs. He may, after all, be needed to mediate between the United States and a new Champion of the General Assembly. When roles are switched, or when there is even a thought that they could be switched, their nature is open to fresh examination.

It is my hope that this book may be of some small help in such a fresh examination. Here I should like to address myself especially to those at the United Nations who will read this book. I know that my Katanga book was read there, by members both of the Secretariat and of national Delegations, and some of the younger among these have been kind enough to say that they found it useful; if they meant 'as a dreadful example' they were already good enough diplomats not to say so. That book contained some inconvenient truths about the United Nations and so does this one, although this time on a more theoretical plane. Assiduity in the relation of inconvenient truths is not usually considered a sign of friendship, and I fear that this book, like its predecessor, may be regarded in some quarters as hostile and damaging to the United Nations. It is not hostile in intent, and—what is more important—it will not be damaging in impact. It will be the reverse of damaging, for it reminds the public which it reaches of the vital, sacred function for which the United Nations was set up; a function which has become somewhat obscured by the dust raised by so many enterprises

of the kind here designated as temporal. The august nature of the United Nations, as the scene of dramatic mediation—prayerful rites for the aversion of doom—is here stressed, for a public which has partly forgotten the role which the United Nations has played, plays, and must continue to play in safeguarding our survival. This is a defence of the essential role of the existing United Nations as against all of the following:

1. The tendency to obscure and distort the essential role of the United Nations—which is a sacred one—for the benefit of various necessary but secondary temporal enterprises in applied peace-keeping.
2. The literalising tendencies of the administrative sub-cult, further confounding sacred and temporal, and
3. The tendency to set up against the existing United Nations a Platonic one, an imaginary 'world government' which would, it is supposed, if it existed, act in the manner desired by the person alluding to it. This is the imaginary organisation which, through Arthur Goldberg, confers its turgid blessing on America's war against Vietnam. In other contexts it serves other and perhaps more admirable purposes, but it always turns on a core of delusion, whereas the existing United Nations, perpetually veiled though it is in illusions, harmless or harmful, has yet a core of sense, in the instinct for survival in the world as it is.

Even so, the defence—some will feel—will do more harm than good, because it violates the official secrecy of the United Nations and because it treats serious matters in an irreverent and even facetious way. The objections are important and obliges us to consider more closely two concepts—secrecy and reverence—which are relevant, in some complex ways to the function and performance of the sacred drama.

On the face of it, the very idea of a 'United Nations secret' is an anomaly. The Secretary-General, and under him the Secretariat, are the servants of the principal organs of the United Nations—the General Assembly and the Security Council—and there is nothing in the Charter to suggest that the servants are authorised to have secrets from their supposed masters. Certainly the framers of the Charter can hardly be supposed to have intended that the Secretariat should systematically keep some of its most important activities secret from one of the permanent members. Yet there is no doubt that this has become the case. Senior Soviet officials in the Secretariat have been systematically kept from access to all important information. My own experience of this phenomenon, in relation to the Congo, is related in *To Katanga and Back*. Mr Tavares de Sá asserts that the 'hallowed system of neutralising all Russians within the

Secretariat has been in operation from the beginnings of the United Nations'[1]; he also explains that a more sophisticated method of keeping the Russians uninformed has succeeded the old crude method of complete bypassing; the new method, dating from the accession of U Thant, consists in 'keeping all Soviet staffers minutely informed of everything that happens within the Secretariat provided that it is of no consequence'.[2]

The justification of this strange procedure is that the Russians, unlike other members of the Secretariat, would be expected to inform officials of their own government of anything of importance learned in the course of their work. Thus they would infringe Staff Regulation 1.5 which states in part:

'Staff members ... shall not communicate to any person any information known to them by reason of their official position which has not been made public, except in the course of their duties or by authorisation of the Secretary-General.'

A Soviet citizen, who is a staff member, and is seen in conversation with a member of the Soviet delegation, is deemed to be probably in breach of this regulation—*if* any information is known to him by reason of his official position. Steps are therefore taken to keep temptation from this weak vessel.

An American citizen, who is a staff member, and is seen in conversation with a member of the United States delegation, is deemed, on the contrary—if he is doing the talking, which is not always the case—either to be communicating information which is already public (a rare case, one would think) or acting in the course of his duties or by authorisation of the Secretary-General. He is assumed to be acting righteously because he is, by nationality, a vessel of salvation.

And in fact, whatever information he may be conveying (provided it is correct), the American staff member will be deemed to have acted 'by authorisation of the Secretary-General'. No Secretary-General, since the beginning, has been in a position to discipline a staff member for divulging a 'United Nations secret' to a United States delegate. The very idea of the United Nations having 'secrets' from the United States would sound strange within the glass palace; the symbiosis between the Secretariat and the host Government makes the idea of such 'secrets' incomprehensible.

The Charter (Article 101, section 1) provides that the staff 'shall be appointed by the Secretary-General under regulations established by the General Assembly'. In the early years, however, the Secretariat functioned under 'provisional regulations' of its own framing. These included a Regulation (5) embodying

[1] *The Play Within the Play*, p. 184.
[2] Ibid, p. 187.

the substance of the present Staff Regulation 1.5. This was the period when, as Mr Lie has observed, the Secretariat was overwhelmingly American in personnel, while its Russian members, as Mr de Sá has observed, were 'neutralised'. The Staff Regulations were approved by the General Assembly at its Sixth Session, in 1951, during the Korean War, at a time when the Assembly (that is, the requisite two-thirds) was entirely subservient to the United States, and when a successful effort was under way, with Mr Lie's help, to make the Secretariat even more reliable from an American point of view. If Staff Regulation 1.5 operates against Soviet citizens in the Secretariat—automatically considered as in potential violation of it—this follows an interpretation which would have been automatic in the days when the Regulations were formed and approved.

All this has ominous implications for the office of Secretary-General. For if the Soviet citizens might reveal to their delegation important facts (known to them in the course of their official duties) without the authorisation of the Secretary-General—and presumably against his wishes—then it appears that the Secretary-General is expected to furnish at least one of the permanent members with something less than a full and true account of the activities of the Secretariat. These activities are 'open' towards one of the superpowers, 'closed' towards the other. And in fact, the 'secrecy against the Russians' principle leads to wider secrecy requirements, since what third parties know, the Russians may learn; also there are certain kinds of information which, if known to, say, Afro-Asian third parties might incense them and thereby 'play into the hands of the Russians'.

The kind of open-at-one-end 'secrecy' actually practised by the Secretariat is, then, a perversion—and also the means of concealing a perversion—of the functions of the Secretariat as originally conceived, and as still popularly imagined. The 'Americanisation' of the Secretariat, bringing with it the principle of 'security against the Russians', dates from the earliest years of the organisation and of the Cold War, and was intensified by the Korean war. This one-sided security was somewhat mitigated—though never really eliminated—by Hammarskjold, but it intensified again, as a result of the Congo imbroglio, and the sad necessities of a fragile credibility.

Since the sacred function of the United Nations is 'to save succeeding generations from the scourge of war', the covert annexation of its Secretariat by *one* of the major potential belligerents, to the detriment of the other, constitutes a major encroachment of the temporal into the sphere of the sacred. That is to say that the values of short-term calculation of sectional advantages have been allowed to prevail over that value which the United Nations was set up to symbolise: the common human determination to survive.

This is not an anti-American or pro-Soviet position on the writer's part: the Soviet Union would also, no doubt, have manipulated the United Nations for its own short-term propaganda purposes, had it been in a position to do so. The vital distinctions are those between sacred and temporal, not between Russian and American.

Disrespect for the kind of secrecy which conceals these transactions from the world—except from the Government of the United States—is not then, disrespect for the United Nations itself; it springs from respect for the sacred function of the United Nations and a desire to cleanse it, in the common interest, from its temporal and sectional accretions. This cannot be done without showing the extent of these accretions.

This is not to say, of course, that secrecy has no legitimate function in the sacred drama. On the contrary, the 'sacred veil' which, according to Burke, must cover 'the origins of all governments' is also an essential part of the apparatus of face-saving and therefore of mediation, and of survival. The face which needs to be saved is in bad shape, and must not be seen in this condition; therefore the Secretary-General must be ready with a veil. The ritual requires the publicised holding of conversations whose content is kept ostentatiously secret, until the formula has been found which in the opinion of the retreating party best preserves his dignity. In terms of the most impressive of existing ritual dramas, the service must be conducted behind the iconostasis, out of sight of the worshippers, until the high moment when the celebrants emerge, make their circuit of the Cathedral, and come back bringing the world the news: Christ is risen; the peace is saved.

14

SACRED SECRECY, a matter for high and solemn occasions, is quite distinct from the temporal and one-sided secrecies which have infested the Secretariat for so long. Even these secrecies cannot be altogether eliminated, but they can be substantially reduced, and above all made less one-sided. The removal from the shoulders of the Secretary-General of responsibility for the execution of local 'peace-keeping' operations would be a very important step in the right direction. Under the kind of arrangement I have suggested, the Co-ordinator and his staff—mostly seconded from the Secretariat—would carry responsibility before the Security Council, and not to the Secretary-General, not only for a given operation, and for any military and other skulduggery in which they might find themselves forced to engage, but also for the 'security' of the operation itself: that is to say for any suppressions of the true, suggestions of the false and occasional downright lies which the success of the operation might require, and for the administrative techniques required to safeguard the credibility of whatever version of events the Co-ordinator might think fit to present 'promptly and fully' to the Security Council or the General Assembly. It is highly desirable to get all this stuff outside the regular functioning of an institution—the Secretariat—which must be thought of as functioning not only with impartiality but also on an exceptionally high moral level. The secular arm will be needed from time to time, but its tasks, necessarily sometimes sordid, should be performed outside the temple—administratively speaking—as far as possible out of earshot, and without in any way contaminating the chief priest.

The other main desirable change—which may be in sight of achievement with the slackening of the Russo-American part of the Cold War—is that all nationalities should be treated as exactly on the same footing in point of reliability. This does not mean adopting the unwise and unrealistic assumption that a Soviet citizen, holding office with the Secretariat, will not inform representatives of his own country of what is going on. It means abandoning the unwise and unrealistic assumption that an American citizen, holding office with the Secretariat, does not inform representatives of his own country of what is going on. Once the execution of peace-keeping operations is excluded from its responsibilities—and excluding also the sphere of 'sacred secrecy' in emergency mediation at the level of the Secretary-General himself—the Secretariat should be able to function in such a way that neither it nor anyone else has anything to fear from its workings being known to all the permanent members.

A certain emphasis on secrecy is likely to continue, in part out of administrative habit; the tendency to 'play at being' a national civil service with its 'State secrets', the rooted feeling of the born official that if what he has committed to a file should become known to the public he would lose some of his strength and virtue. An organisation whose functions are so largely those of ritual is a 'play organisation' in the sense that Huizinga uses that term in *Homo Ludens* and Huizinga points out that 'The exceptional and special point of play is most tellingly illustrated by the fact that it loves to surround itself with an air of secrecy'.[1] More substantial than all this is the fact that governments may often wish their communications with the Secretariat to be kept secret, not so much for fear of other governments—they know that the American Government for one will know immediately anything of any importance that they may confide to the Secretariat—but for fear that publication might embarrass them before the public in their own country. The Secretariat, being responsible to organs composed of representatives of governments, is acting within the sphere assigned to it when it does what it can to assure this kind of secrecy.

The critique—and the breach—of prevailing forms of United Nations secrecy, can therefore be combined with full respect for the kinds of secrecy which the United Nations actually needs in order to perform the functions envisaged by the Charter. Secrecy designed to cover transactions not envisaged by the Charter, and potentially detrimental to its main purpose, deserves no respect.

The question of reference is in some ways related to that of secrecy. Reverence is appropriate to the essential function of the United Nations: the opening words of the Preamble are such as to evoke reverence in all who have children, or hope to have them. Reverence is also appropriate towards the concepts of the Security Council, and the General Assembly and towards the office of Secretary-General, for these are the symbols of the prayer raised in the Preamble.

Just as respect for the theatre not only does not preclude, but actually requires, harsh judgements of certain performances, and as belief in the Church requires protest against intrusions of scandalously temporal considerations into its life, so reverence for the sacred purpose declared in the opening words of the Preamble requires irreverence towards the temporal encroachments which menace the attainment of that purpose. There is of course, a tendency to present, and even to think of, these temporal encroachments as constituting the United Nations itself. The Secretariat, with its deep-rooted complicities with the policies and practices of one permanent member, its administrative cult of 'established practice' based on the precedents of peace-keeping operations, conducted mainly on behalf of that

[1] *Homo Ludens*, p. 12.

member, has no right to think of itself, or to ask others to think of it, as *being* the United Nations. It is a part of the United Nations which has been to a very large extent diverted from its original and sacred purpose, to serve temporal and sectional ends. The 'established practice', to which it is so proud to cling, is in great part the record of its corruptions. What it needs is not conformity with precedent, nor yet the rehabilitation of its 'image', the refurbishing of the pious assumption that it is a body of 'neutral men'. What it needs is a reformation.

15

THERE ARE, of course, many officials within the Secretariat itself who are conscious of the need for a reformation, and who are scandalised, in particular, by the significance of the 'keep it dark from the Russians' side of a supposedly impartial 'international civil service'. Mr Tavares de Sá, in *The Play within the Play*, notes, not without irony, the existence of such officials; he calls them 'the internationalists'. It is the measure of the extent to which the Secretariat has been diverted from its purpose as originally proclaimed, that one rather small group of its members should be distinguished as 'the internationalists'; as if 'internationalism' in the United Nations were some odd, private quirk.

The hand of 'the internationalists' should have been strengthened by some recent trends in international affairs. The slackening of the Cold War, as between the Soviet Union and the United States, should operate, together with the fact that no one country can any longer be sure of obtaining automatically the legitimation of the General Assembly, to allow the Secretariat to gravitate back towards the centre. U Thant himself has earned the reputation of being an 'internationalist'. Yet the composition of the Secretariat, and its traditions, are such that progress has been slow. Mr de Sá's description of the evolution, under Thant, of the 'secrecy against Russia' policy from one of general bypassing to one of 'snowing under' has a depressing ring. If this is true—and I have no reason to doubt it—the atmosphere in the Secretariat, in this most important respect, is still that of some ill-run prep-school in which the boys are encouraged by some of the senior staff to play silly tricks on the French master. At this level we are far indeed, both from the Charter and its Preamble, and from any kind of drama, publicly presentable.

Financial questions are usually a major barrier to reformation, and here again the United Nations conforms to an ecclesiastical model. The Soviet Union refuses to pay its share of certain 'peace-keeping' enterprises which it holds to have been illegally set up (i.e. by the General Assembly, as in the case of UNEF in Egypt) or illegally conducted, as in the case of the Congo. In the latter case, it would be surprising if the Soviet Union did agree to pay 'its share' of expenditure which covered, among other matters, the eviction costs of its own Embassy (those 5,000,000 francs paid on behalf of the U.N. to Joseph Mobutu on 10 September, 1960). As France also refuses to pay for enterprises which it did not support, and from which it considers it derived no benefit, the United Nations is heavily in deficit. For help with this deficit it can only look to the United States. The United States, having exercised predominant influence—in varying directions—over the course of the United Nations operations in the Congo, and having, through that operation, inflicted a major political and diplomatic defeat on the Soviet Union in Africa, derives further political benefits, in the form of strengthened influence over the United Nations, by being not only the major financial supporter of this enterprise, and of the United Nations, but also the Power to which the United Nations must look for help with its continuing difficulties. Just as the political conjuncture seems about to free the Secretariat from its one-sided servitude, the financial conjuncture—the result of the politics of the past—drags it back again towards its old status.

There is, as we have seen, a very strong case for insulating the Secretary-General from executive responsibility for peace-keeping operations; there is also a strong case for a new assessment of the financial basis of peace-keeping operations. There is no basis in the Charter for the notion that members are generally liable for their proportionate share of the cost of such operations as are recommended by the General Assembly. It would be more in keeping, both with the Charter and with reality, for the costs of such operations to be borne by those states which support or accept the recommendation in question. Even in the case of Security Council decisions, it seems desirable to take peace-keeping expenditure outside the regular budget, leaving the bulk of it to be borne by those permanent members which vote in favour of the operation. This would not alter the substantial basis of such operations, which even under present arrangements will not take place unless at least one major Power judges them sufficiently in accordance with its national interest to take part in them (Korea), or give them financial, technical and logistic support (Congo). To place their financing on the same voluntary basis as participation in peace-keeping, and to relieve the Secretary-General of executive responsibility for such operations, would tend to restore the United Nations to its true spiritual role—of providing a rite legitimising action by its members—without requiring it to assume either moral or financial responsibility for the executive actions of the secular arm. It would also tend to restore to the United Nations both its moral authority and its financial independence—that is to say a position of reliance on its regular dues, and not on special hand-outs.

The Charter, of course, envisaged (in Chapter VII) neither a 'voluntary' system, nor the 'Congo' system of a special levy, but a system under which 'the Security Council'—meaning the armed forces of the permanent members—might 'take such action by air, sea or land forces as may be necessary to maintain or restore international peace and security'.[1] Because of the Cold

[1] Article 43.

War, and the failure to set up the Military Staff Committee provided for in Article 47, the institutions through which the Security Council could act in this way never came into being, and the Security Council has never had actual material power. This being so, only a voluntary system—of forces supplied by members for an enterprise legitimised by the United Nations—has been possible. The financing of such enterprises on a voluntary basis is as compatible with the Charter as a special levy—and much more conducive to the purposes of the Charter.

In the meantime, however, the United Nations is weighed down by a past of biased activities (for one of the superpowers against the other) and bad debts, and a present of 'established practice' leading to more of the same. To reform all this from within is not easy. U Thant resembles in some ways some reform-minded Pope, contending against the smooth conservatism of his Curia, the weight of past and present temporal commitments, the indebtedness of his institution, and the indispensable and intolerable generosity of one great patron. Nor need one look to the past for this analogy. The 'secular Pope' on the East River, and the acknowledged Pope by the Tiber are in a similar position *now*, and their utterances are in remarkable harmony. To both, men look for moral leadership, in the cause of peace. Both are obviously troubled in mind and conscience by the long war which the greatest of the industrialised Powers is waging against an Asian peasantry. Yet both head institutions which are intimately related to that great Power. American contributions sustain the Vatican as well as the United Nations. The Pope prays for peace, but neglects an opportunity to retire Cardinal Spellman who prays for American victory. U Thant strives to mediate from within an institution deeply permeated by the power of *one* of the parties, between whom he seeks to mediate, through all its main organs: a Security Council from which China is kept out for the benefit of an American satellite: a General Assembly which annually ratifies that transaction: and a Secretariat in which American citizens exert great influence, while Soviet citizens are flouted and impotent. In this situation it is not surprising if the voices of both U Thant and Pope Paul have seemed to sound a note of pathos rather than one of authority.

In the case of U Thant, and considering the limitations of the institution for which he speaks, what is remarkable is that he has been able to throw his weight discreetly but unequivocally against the United States policy in Vietnam: that is, against the prolongation of the present policy, in the most sensitive area, of the most powerful member of the United Nations. Inevitably of course he is taxed with having compromised his mediatory function by so doing. It appears, however, that he has found mediation to be impossible in present circumstances, and has had recourse to public intercession both in the hope of speeding on the time of mediation and of reinforcing the moral authority of the Secretary-General for when that time comes. From the point of view of a future historian it may appear that by this stand—unheeded though it has been so far—U Thant has done more to strengthen, in the long term, the moral authority of the United Nations than either of his more spectacular predecessors were able to do. In terms of the present discussion, his sense of the requirements of the sacred outweighs his lack of a dramatic sense.

16

AT THE time of writing, the Secretary-General's appeals are disregarded, and the United Nations has found itself unable even to express an opinion on the subject of his appeals.

A certain historical perspective is necessary here, if one is not to despair of the United Nations altogether, or—what amounts to the same thing—start babbling about Charter revision, 'weighted voting', 'abolishing the veto' and the other paraphernalia of the Platonic United Nations. The great merit of the curious institution on the East River is that it has proved itself to be possible by actually existing; the governments of the world (except China, the Koreas, the Vietnams and the Germanies) have been able to come together, under its rules, and perform ceremonies which do provide a kind of communion for humanity as a whole, as the Papacy did for Christendom, and the shrine at Delphi for the Hellenic world. A shrine in a real world will always be manipulated to some extent by the rich and powerful, without however losing *all* its virtue for that. One of the greatest benefactors of the Panhellenic shrine and sanctuary at Delphi was, appropriately, Croesus, the Lydian king and plutocrat. 'The Lydian kings were renowned in later ages for their bountiful generosity to Apollo and the oft-quoted prophecies which the Pythia [the oracle of Apollo] had given them.'[1] Croesus helped the shrine out of its financial difficulties, and its resolutions, 'or prophecies' as they were called, were helpful to his cause. His contributions seem to have been elicited in part by sincere belief in the sacred function of Apollo's shrine, and in part by rational calculation of the short-term, temporal advantage which he could extract from it in relation to temporal politics:

'The vast munificence of Croesus' dedications cannot be explained entirely as a disinterested tribute to the Pythian Apollo. Croesus may, even must, have believed in the truth and importance of Delphi. But Delphi must have given him some special cause for choosing it as an object of his generosity. . . . In deciding to make war on Persia Croesus would have wished not only for the backing of the Greeks of Asia Minor, whom he had made his subjects, but also for the active support of allies, from mainland Greece, if he could secure them. . . . In persuading the co-operation of Greek allies, Delphi might prove of peculiar value. A favourable prophecy from the Pythia, some encouragement to the Greeks to assist, and the task of making Sparta support him would be possible. . . . One cannot doubt that the oracle's reply was strongly favourable without the suspicious ambiguities which the later versions contained. On

[1] H. W. Parke and D. E. W. Wormell, *The Delphic Oracle*, Oxford, 1946, p. 126; all the subsequent quotations on Delphi are taken from this fascinating work.

the Delphians the seemingly boundless wealth of the Lydian monarchy must have made an overpowering impression. Gold at this period was very scarce in Greece and a ruler who could dispense hoards in bounties must have seemed the master of invincible resources. Persia or even Media can have been scarcely more than a name. Thence an unqualified backing of Croesus must have seemed the only sensible policy.'[2]

Sparta, like many another country, summoned by a similar prophesy from another shrine to war in Korea nearly 2,500 years later, supported the war in principle but 'used her native caution and did not send any actual assistance'.[3] There the direct parallel ends, however. The Persians won the war and 'the fall of Croesus was followed by a long period of pro-Persian prophesying.'[4]

Other states, in Delphi's long history, were able to exercise similar control over the area of the shrine and over its prophecies. The account of the predominant influence of Philip of Macedon over the Delphic Amphictyony—defined as 'a league of states surrounding a religious centre'—strikes a particularly modern and Unosian note:

'He controlled not merely the two votes of his own, but through his hold over Thessaly and Northern Greece he could also count on the double votes of the Thessalians, Delphians, Perrhaetian-Dolopes, Magnesians, Aenians and Malians and the single vote of Doris while Eastern and Western Locris must have been open to pressure from him. Hence Philip could be sure of a clear majority on any issue that came before the Council.'[5]

Granted this general context it is hardly surprising to learn that the 'Delphic oracle consistently supported Philip against Athens as the champion of Apollo's cause'. In Athens, Demosthenes devised the most succinct formula ever produced to describe the manipulation of a sacred office for temporal and sectional purposes. 'The Pythia,' he said, 'is philippising.'

The Pythia, like the Pope and the United Nations, spent much of her time philippising, for one Philip or another. This helped to weaken the sacred power of Delphi—Parke and Wormell point out that 'sceptics in later ages quoted the phrase [of Demosthenes] with damaging effect. . . .'[6] None the less, over a long period, the Pythia seems to have played a useful part in the development of Hellenic civilisation, in the refinement of human manners and in particular in the substitution of rituals

---

[2] *The Delphic Oracle*, pp. 135–6.
[3] Ibid, p. 136.
[4] Ibid, p. 418.
[5] Ibid, p. 233.
[6] Ibid, p. 237.

for the shedding of human blood. One phrase of Parke and Wormell about the Pythia is as applicable to the U.N. at its best in its sacred functioning, as 'the Pythia is philippising' is to the U.N. at its temporal worst. 'The Pythia,' they say, 'appears as a moderating influence to prevent the application of extreme measures in the heat of the moment. . . .'[7]

Their account suggests also that the sacred function of the shrine—when it was not obscured by philippising—was inspired by the same spirit as the Preamble to the Charter: 'the special importance of bloodguilt in Delphic tradition suggests rather that the Pythian Apollo was one of the first deities strongly to discountenance the shedding of human blood'.[8] In its more routine functioning also, this account of Delphi presents striking similarities with the United Nations:

'. . . the influence of the Delphic oracle was something more than the sum of its responses. The mere fact that Delphi provided a centre for enquiry on many subjects was of incalculable importance to the Greek world. The chief tendency of each state was towards forming itself into a separate unit, and these monads were not easily led to have any common contact. Here Delphi played a remarkable part in Greek civilisation, as for much of their history all the city states . . . might meet at Delphi on similar terms and transact the same kind of business in their dealings with Apollo. This common activity showed itself in much more than merely the consultation of the oracle. For instance the Pythia, so far as we know, was comparatively rarely approached on questions of arbitration, but inscriptions reveal that Delphi was often the scene of settlements by arbitration between states without any consulting of Apollo.'[9]

In a similar way, the United Nations provides opportunities for continuous contact, and unpublicised adjustments of matters in dispute. Indeed states which are publicly inveighing against each other on the floor of the Assembly may at the same time be working out a compromise behind the scenes. This was the case with Greece and Turkey at (at least) one stage of the Cyprus dispute. These cases also sometimes leave their 'inscriptions' in the form of agreed and unanimous resolutions.

Messrs. Parke and Wormell warn, however, against assimilating Delphi too closely to a later institution. In quoting their comparisons between Delphi and the Vatican (below) I have inserted, in italics between brackets, my own comparisons with the United Nations:

'There is,' they note, 'a temptation to exaggerate the central-

---

[7] *The Delphic Oracle*, p. 359.
[8] Ibid, p. 364.
[9] Ibid, p. 416.

ising power of Delphi by attributing too much positive influence to it. For example, it has often been compared to the Papacy, and some of its activities exhibit a curious similarity of function. The control of colonisation (*compare the U.N.'s role in decolonisation*) has been likened to Pope Alexander VI's partition of the New World between Spain and Portugal. The Pythia too could occasionally issue a kind of excommunication against particular individuals or cities (*the U.N.'s 'brandings' of the People's Republic of China, the Soviet Union, etc.*) and her judgements on questions of cult, particularly on the recognition of heroes, closely resemble the decisions of canonisation. (*There is no real U.N. parallel to this. The U.N. has already its own roll of martyrs, headed by Bernadotte and Hammarskjold, but that is another matter.*) Even the Delphic claim that their oracle was "without deceit" answered to the dogma of Infallibility (*not merely are the decisions of the Security Council binding on all member nations (Article 25) but the Organisation has conferred on itself the right to ensure that* non-Members *act in accordance with the 'Principles' which it has devised in pursuit of its 'Purposes' (Article 2, section 6)*). But these interesting analogies conceal the fact that the power of Delphi, rested on a very different basis from that of the Papacy. If to press the analogy further, Oenomaus of Gadara (*author of a disillusioned and sceptical work about the Apollonian prophecies—compare Mr Tavares de Sá*) was a would-be Protestant reformer, there was still no Catholic Church behind the Pythia, and Delphi was not the centre of an organised religious system.'[10]

It is right to stress the difference, yet its existence does not invalidate the 'curious similarity of function between certain activities of the two institutions'— or the continuing human needs to which this similarity points. But the difference which Parke and Wormell stress, as existing between Delphi and the Papacy, brings home to us the fact that the United Nations is in this respect closer to its older model. The United Nations, like Delphi, is an international shrine, without a Church—though the United Nations regional information offices, working together with local United Nations Associations, do represent an aspiration towards organising a world-wide communion of believers in the United Nations; Hammarskjold's ambitions for the Organisation lay in this direction.

At the United Nations the equivalent of Apollo is Man: of prophecies, resolutions. Men listen to the voice from this shrine as to the voice of Man: what there is of a collective will to survive. The voice comes through strange channels: those of governments, most of which have only the vaguest claim to represent 'the will of the people of Tsetseland'. Yet this too has its fitness.

[10] *The Delphic Oracle*, pp. 416–17.

These men do not represent 'the people of Tsetseland' but they do represent the conditions of survival in Tsetseland at a given moment in time. These conditions may include subservience to the will of a foreign power, or a feudal prince, or an oil company, but whatever they are, these are the conditions of the time and place. If the political conditions change overtly—if, for example, there is a revolution, or a coup d'état, the death of a potentate, a palace revolt, or even, in the case of a small number of countries, a change by election—then the representation of the country will change also (except in the special case of China) and so probably will the pattern of its vote and speeches at the United Nations. So the collective prophesying on the East River will take on a different inflection. If it is the government of a great country that has changed—by, for example, the death of Stalin in 1953, or the inauguration of John Kennedy in 1960—then the change is audible to all. If it is a small country—like, say, Iraq—the change will be faint, but perceptible to an experienced ear (for example, that of one of the 'arm-twisters' of the U.S. Permanent Mission). When a new set of political survivors take the floor in place of others who have failed to survive—always politically and often also physically—it is a signal that the conditions of political survival on a part of the planet have significantly changed, changing also in some degree the character of the drama of survival at the United Nations. This is entirely appropriate, for the drama is one of survival under actual conditions, through a series of often sordid, brutal and unjust 'nows', not one of survival in ideal conditions of world government based on universal democracy—a task that can be left to the Platonic United Nations.

It is therefore a matter of fundamental principle that only survivors should take part in the drama of survival. This is why the seating of a Chiang Kai Shek delegate in the place of China is the great sin of the United Nations: the sin against survival. The Russians are in the habit of calling this delegation 'the political corpse of Chiang Kai Shek' and of drawing attention to the fact that it is 'stinking' and 'ought to be buried'. This is not in good taste, but it is true. The rites of survival cannot be duly performed in the presence of a corpse. The sacred drama cannot discharge one of its essential functions—the acting out of aggression—if that great country around which the greatest charges of aggression have accumulated, is represented by something which it has rejected. The drama, thus staged, can excite only derision and contempt in the country concerned; for the Chinese, the Pythia never does anything but philippise. But for others too, the sacred drama, debased in this particular, loses much of its authority. Its pacifying potential is therefore lowered: to less than nothing in one great area, and to some extent everywhere.

By this, as by other temporal intrusions on the sacred functions, the margin within which humanity survives is made narrower than it need be.

The philippisings of the ancient Pythia were tolerable; neither Croesus nor the Persians, neither Philip nor the Athenians, had the power to destroy humanity; the shrine had not the function of averting a general doom; it was operating within a wide margin, disposing of long reaches of time. Its specific sacred function, the commutation of blood-guilt through ritual, was not paralysed by its philippising, though it may well have been impaired. It was possible for men, to some extent, to separate its 'political' from its 'religious' utterances. It played its part in the history of civilisation, and gradually faded away. *The History of the Delphic Oracle* refers to its 'last utterances', the answer given, through the quaestor Oribasius, to Julian the Apostate who sought to revive the oracle:

'Tell the king, the fairwrought hall has fallen to the ground. No longer has Phoebus a hut, nor a prophetic laurel, nor a spring that speaks. The water of speech even is quenched.'

17

IF IN our time the fair-wrought hall by the East River should fall to the ground, our civilisation would be likely to have fallen with it. The religious and the political can no longer be separated: the sacred function of this place is a political one; the rituals for the aversion of the doom are political rituals. This is why philippising, tolerable enough in the ancient system, has become enormously dangerous in the present one. The modern Philip, when he manipulates the United Nations for a short-term political end, is neglecting his own most vital long-term interest: his share in the common interest in survival. His life, as well as ours, may depend in an emergency on the level of the drama's reserve of authority—that which makes it possible to 'bow' to it without loss of dignity. Every philippising is a drain on that reserve. The case of China is the clearest and most ominous demonstration of this.

The present essay was conceived, not primarily in a 'reforming' spirit, but as part of a continuing effort to understand the United Nations better, stemming from a growing conviction that I did not understand it very well, and that neither did most of those whom I had known (or read) who worked with or in the institution (or who wrote about it). The source of the misunderstanding, I have come to believe, lies in the combination of the 'literalising' and 'administrative' tendencies—taking the 'Organisation' seriously in the wrong way—with the Platonic 'world government' conception. This combination tends to produce a conviction that the United Nations needs to be 'strengthened'—that is, to acquire administrative authority—and that this is most likely to be achieved through successive 'peace-keeping' enterprises, gradually enhancing the authority of the Secretary-General. Convictions of this kind are quite prevalent among 'good United Nations people', both inside and outside the Secretariat, and are often associated with a certain contempt for the more theatrical 'General Assembly' side of United Nations activity. These people are, I believe, right in their sense of the importance of the United Nations, and of the need to strengthen it; wrong in their idea of what it is in the United Nations that can be strengthened, and of how to strengthen it. The main source of confusion has been the mirage of 'world government'; with the wistful hope that the United Nations, with a little shoving, will somehow begin to turn into this. Not that the idea that there may be some day a world government is necessarily illusory; if humanity tries to begin to solve the problems of class war and race war, to stabilise its population at an optimum level, and feed and clothe and educate it, then it is probable that effective world institutions of control will also be beginning to emerge by consent. World government by conquest—the principal method

by which human beings have historically achieved larger administrative units—is also a theoretical possibility, but could not be attained without the violent deaths of many millions: this is obviously not the kind of 'world government' that those who most use that term have in mind. World government by consent is, obviously, an interesting but remote ideal; even those in (say) the United States who talk most piously about 'strengthening the United Nations' do not seriously intend that the United States should itself now give up any part of its sovereignty: they just mean that it would be nice if other countries did so. 'The zealots of world government,' wrote T.S. Eliot, '... may, without knowing it, take for granted that the final world-culture will be simply an extension of that to which they belong themselves.'[1] Arnold Toynbee tells us how dangerous nationalism is, and that world government *must* be achieved. Yes, but in the meantime? It is not really very helpful to tell us that nationalism 'in the atomic age . . . is a death-wish'[2] or to place 'the 114 present states-members of the United Nations . . . at the bottom of our political marking-list'.[3] It is not in our power to shake out of a box a brand new set of member-states, free from nationalism, and ready to cede their sovereignty to a Toynbeean world-government.

Moreover, the bent of mind of the most peremptory 'world government now' people may not be as conducive to peace as they assume it to be. Their enthusiasm for the very large has something inhuman about it. Thus Dr. Toynbee provides us with the following moral 'balance-sheet' of the Mongol empire: 'The Mongols in the thirteenth century of the Christian era committed genocide almost on the scale on which it has been committed by the Nazis in our Western society in our day. On the other side of the balance sheet, we must enter to the Mongols' credit the fact that they succeeded in establishing, and in maintaining thereafter for a century, a would be world-state that came nearer to being world-wide than any other that has been established either before or since, hitherto.'[4] It is to the discredit of the Mongols that they (supposedly) practised genocide; it is to their credit, however, that they put themselves in a position to practise it over a very wide area for quite a long period. We are not told what the final reading of the Mongol balance sheet is after that credit entry; the passage does, however, imply that the achievement of a real and lasting world government would be considered as outweighing, in the Toynbeean moral balance,

---

[1] *Notes towards the Definition of Culture*, p. 135.
[2] *Change and Habit: the Challenge of our Time* (1966), p. 112.
[3] Ibid, p. 24.
[4] Ibid, p. 25.

notable amounts of oppression of the governed, though perhaps not genocide, or not much genocide. Those who fear that any kind of world government that could conceivably emerge in our time might well be such as to make us regret 'the international anarchy of the nation-States' are not likely to be reassured by the trend of Dr Toynbee's argument here.

'Scratch an enthusiast for "world government now" and you will find an imperialist.' Those who are inclined to reject that proposition should consider the career of Mr Cord Meyer. Mr Cord Meyer started out as a 'world government idealist'. In *Peace or Anarchy* he wrote: 'Disarmament must be enforced by law and the possession of war-making power by national governments prohibited.'[5] 'Either some measure of world government will be achieved by voluntary consent or our particular civilisation will be destroyed.'[6] Finding that disarmament did not seem to be about to be enforced by law, or world government about to emerge, Mr Meyer joined the Central Intelligence Agency of the United States and eventually came to head that section of it which waged the Cold War, on the intellectual and cultural fronts, by covertly financing the activities of 'anti-communist but liberal' institutions and individuals inside and outside the United States. There is no question here of impugning Mr Meyer's sincerity. *Peace or Anarchy* is one of the best formulations of the 'world government now' position and there is every reason to believe that he meant what he said; the book is dedicated to his brother who was killed in the Second World War, in which Mr Meyer himself lost an eye. Nor is his adherence to the C.I.A. inconsistent with this earlier position; rather, the point I would make here is that it flows logically from the earlier position. If you say *either* peace through world government *or* the anarchy of competing nationalisms, and you find there is not going to be world government, then it is quite logical to serve whichever nationalism you think most benign, which will usually be that of your own nation. From the ideal of 'peace through world government' Mr Meyer falls back on the more practical objective of the *Pax Americana* which—extending through the whole of the Western hemisphere, Oceania, Australasia, South-East Asia, large and increasing areas of the African continent and most of Western Europe, including the British Isles—is the most nearly world-wide system that now exists. For a disappointed 'world government-by-voluntary-consent' man, to serve this system is as logical as it was for a disappointed 'world revolution' man in the 1930s to serve the national policies of the Soviet Union. And some of course like Mr Jay

[5] *Peace or Anarchy* (1947), p. 151.
[6] Ibid, p. 233.

UNANSWERED QUESTIONS

Saigon 1966
VHD Vien Hoa Dao (Unified Buddhist Church's Institute for the Execution of the Dharma)

Saigon, 1966

NIGERIA'S LEADER

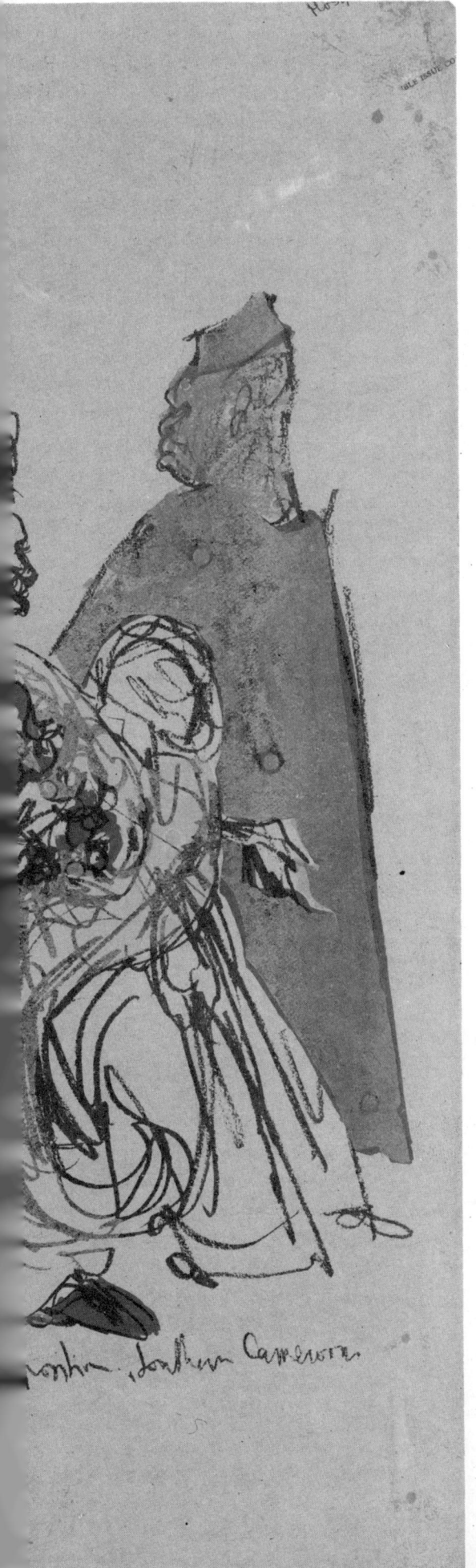

Page from Topolski's Chronicle 1959

NIGERIA

Lagos, Nigeria.

Pearl River

Lovestone have served both sides with the same ruthless and total commitment.

The peremptory, impatient 'all or nothing' style of the world-government people—and the mental attitude and possible future options that underlie this style—are not likely at present to contribute to the preservation of world peace. That insistence on the need for urgent and drastic change in the *structure*[7] of international relations—an insistence which certainly helped to set up the United Nations—can do little now to help us make the best use of the actual possibilities of that institution.

The problem is how best to use the existing United Nations—made up of the people who make it up, and who do not want to submit themselves to a world-government—so that it may increase, as much as possible, our chances of survival in the present world—a world not only of nationalism, but imperialism, class-war, race-war, and the population explosion—and that our children may have some hopes of seeing a better human society. If we cannot avoid utter disaster, by the ways we use the present, highly imperfect 'machinery', the perfect kind will never come into being.

It is argued here that the *theatrical* United Nations, the United Nations of verbal nationalist contending, of ritual confrontations and ritual retreats, of dramatic supplications and sanctified concessions, represents, under the nuclear balance of terror, our best hope of reducing danger in recurring crises. It is also argued that a better understanding of this—of the nature of the sacred drama—can itself improve our chances, by leading, for example, to a recognition of the need to protect the mediating function of the Secretary-General—for his *deus ex machina* emergency appearances—from the contagion of executive peace-keeping responsibilities; and the need also for major powers to realise their interest in protecting a moral authority which they are likely one day to have to invoke, to cover a retreat, or legitimise a salutary but inglorious inaction.

In short, an attempt at a deeper understanding of what is essential in the United Nations, induces a conviction of the need for a reformation in its usages: not Charter revision towards world government, but a more effective use of the existing Charter in the world we actually live in.

---

[7] As distinct from reform of *practice*, within existing structures, which is urgently needed.

18

'... In myth and ritual,' wrote Johan Huizinga, 'the great instinctive forces of civilised life have their origin: law and order, commerce and profit, craft and art, poetry, wisdom and science. All are rooted in the primaeval soil of play.'[1] He stresses the serious implications of play, the social importance of the ancient sacred drama: 'The participants in the rite are convinced that the action actualises and effects a definite beatification, bringing about an order of things higher than that in which they customarily live. All the same this 'actualisation by representation' still retains the formal characteristics of play in every respect... A sacred space, a temporarily real world of its own, has been expressly hedged off for it. But with the end of the play its effect is not lost; rather it continues to shed its radiance on the ordinary world outside, a wholesome influence working security, order and prosperity for the whole community until the sacred play-session comes round again.'[2]

Writing on the eve of the Second World War—his foreword is dated June, 1938—Huizinga was deeply disturbed by what he regarded as the ominous disappearance of the 'play' element from international affairs. In his chapter 'Play and War' he writes:

'The primitive ideal of honour and nobility—rooted in that first of sins, Superbia—is superseded in more advanced phases of civilisation by the ideal of justice, or rather, this ideal attaches itself to it and, however miserably put into practice, henceforth becomes the recognised and desiderated norm of human society, which has now grown from a huddle of clans and tribes to an association of great nations and States. The law "of nations" derives from the agonistic sphere as the consciousness, or voice of conscience, which says: "This goes against honour, is against the rules." Once a thorough-going system of international obligations based on ethics has been developed, there is hardly any room for the agonistic element in the relations of States, for the system tries to sublimate the instinct of political struggle in a true sense of justice and equity. In a community of States bound by one international law universally recognised there is, in theory, no reason for agonistic warfare among its members. Even so, such a community will not have lost all the features of a play-community. Its principle of reciprocal rights, its diplomatic forms, its mutual obligations in the matter of honouring treaties and, in the event of war, officially abrogating peace, all bear a formal resemblance to play-rules inasmuch as they are only binding while the game itself—i.e. the need for order in

[1] *Homo Ludens: A Study of the Play-Element in Culture*, Beacon Press, Boston. All the quotations from Huizinga which follow are taken from the English translation published by the Beacon Press.

[2] Ibid, pp. 14–15.

human affairs—is recognised. We might, in a purely formal sense, call all society a game, if we bear in mind that this game is the living principle of all civilisation.

'Things have now come to such a pass that the system of international law is no longer acknowledged, or observed, as the very basis of culture and civilised living. As soon as one member or more of a community of States virtually denies the binding character of international law and, either in practice or in theory, proclaims the interests and power of its own group—be it nation, party, class, church or whatsoever else—as the sole norm of its political behaviour, not only does the last vestige of the immemorial play-spirit vanish but with it any claim to civilisation at all. Society then sinks down to the level of the barbaric, and original violence retakes its ancient rights.

'The inference from all this is that in the absence of the play-spirit civilisation is impossible.'[3]

Huizinga does not even mention the League of Nations, which is perhaps not surprising, considering the date at which he was writing. The League, thoroughly 'philippised' from its inception by France and Britain, had fallen into discredit, following the half-hearted and soon-abandoned attempt of these powers to use it to legitimise action against Mussolini, over Ethiopia, in 1936. On that occasion the use made of the League was utterly destructive of its moral authority, and therefore of its essence. First, that moral authority had been solemnly invoked and thereby exalted in the eyes of the nations. Sir Samuel Hoare had announced to the League Assembly in September, 'the unswerving fidelity of the British Government to the League and all it stands for and support for the collective maintenance of the Covenant in its entirety, and particularly for steady and collective resistance to all acts of unprovoked aggression'. France had also, though with less enthusiasm, agreed to fulfil the obligations of the Covenant. The Council of the League had found on October, 1936, that Italy was in breach of Article 12 of the Covenant and was therefore 'deemed to have committed an act of war against all other Members of the League'. A large majority of the Assembly endorsed this a few days later. Sanctions were voted, but care was taken that they should be such as not to cause serious annoyance. For 'on the very day before he spoke in the Assembly, Hoare had agreed with Laval that the sanctions applied should only be such as would not lead to war'. Mussolini conquered Ethiopia and the moral authority of the League was in ruins. It was as if the United States, having obtained the required resolutions on Korea from the Security Council and General Assembly, had then refrained from action—or as if the

[3] *Homo Ludens*, pp. 100–1.

United States, having no intention of intervening in Hungary, had got the Assembly to legitimise intervention. It was the worst and most irresponsible form of philippising—philippising for the purpose of deriving a short term political advantage by means of an empty bluff. When the deception was exposed, suspension of disbelief was no longer possible. This drama lost all aura of the sacred and lost its audience also. Humanity's margin of safety had been drastically and irresponsibly diminished.

The United Nations, despite all its vicissitudes, has never been completely stripped of its moral authority, as the League was. If it too has often been made to philippise, it has at least not been made to suffer the humiliation of having its authority invoked for purposes of a bluff, which was called. The United States in fact has used its predominant influence over the United Nations with a greater sense of responsibility than the British and French governments showed in the use of their authority over the League (although exercises like the exhibition of the 'powerlessness of the United Nations' in order to divert attention from the United States decision not to intervene in Hungary in 1956 did damage the moral authority of the United Nations). Partly as a result of this, but more because of the expanded membership and the dynamics of Cold War competition in the underdeveloped world, the United Nations, having now outlasted the total life-span of the League, still shows greater vitality than the League ever did.

It can, I think, be justly claimed for the United Nations that it has restored to international life that element of 'play'—in Huizinga's sense—whose disappearance he felt to be so ominous in 1938. It does not, of course, represent the 'thorough-going system of international obligations based on ethics' for which he hoped and it does leave 'room for the agonistic element in the relations of states'. In fact it is precisely its main function to provide room in which this element can have play, with the minimum danger to world peace. This function is in complete conformity with the general ideas of *Homo Ludens*, and it is at first sight strange that Huizinga did not explore the possibilities of his theory of 'play' for international relations. There is, indeed, a contradiction in his handling of the subject. On the one hand, he felt that the disappearance of 'play' from international relations was a sinister development. On the other he himself felt obliged to require 'play' to disappear—or almost disappear—in favour of a 'true sense of justice and equity' within 'a thorough-going system of international obligations based on ethics'.

Homo Ludens is a splendid book, and Huizinga's conception of play is a dazzling and liberating one. This passage, however, contains an anomaly and an intrusion. Where after all has *homo ludens* gone? The participants in this ultimate virtuous Areopagus hardly belong to the same species as those whose activities Huizinga describes in the rest of his book, and whom we recognise with a delight to which approval is irrelevant. These new playless—or only dimly and vestigially playful—beings conform to specifications for denizens of the Platonic League of Nations, world government by agreement, the City of God. Their deliberations, admirable as they are assumed to be, hardly seem to concern us much. Although the most successful national parliaments are considerably more advanced and sophisticated in their workings than any international body yet in existence, no national parliament, even in the most advanced countries, has ever looked like attaining 'a thoroughgoing system of . . . obligations based on ethics'. An American Congressman recognised the other day (March 1967) that there was considerable truth in a letter he had received from a constituent who considered that Congressmen generally 'were just a bunch of bums'. This is probably no more—or less—true about the American Congress than about other successful parliaments: and no more, or less, true about parliamentary representatives than about their constituents (including those who write them abusive letters). Judged by the standards of any 'thorough-going system of ethics' which human beings have framed, for their amusement and self-torment, humanity itself is just a big 'bunch of bums', and any more or less representative institution, national or international, which it generates, always turns out to be a little 'bunch of bums'. The ideas of a virtuous world-government, sage international federation or simply the conduct of relations between sovereign states on the basis of 'a true sense of equity and justice', requires as a preliminary that humanity shall have become radically different from what it is. *Homo ludens*, calling himself *homo sapiens*, is required to transform himself into *homo bonus solemnis*. This change either will occur, or it will not. If it will not, then world-government of the voluntary and virtuous kind will not occur either, and neither will any of its analogues—world federation freely entered into, voluntary acceptance of an international rule of law, the Charter 'without the veto', legal abolition of war, complete and general disarmament, 'and the Lord knows what'.

In a valuable recent work, *The Cold War as History*, Louis J. Halle has some pertinent comment on such theoretically radical proposals, as remedies for present conditions:

'These possibilities (for reducing the danger of atomic war) surely did not, however, include immediate world government or some act whereby war was abolished, both of these being abstract concepts from the nominal world of law without adequate correspondence to the real world in which the danger presented itself. (The legal abolition of war, for example, would not really abolish war any more than the legal abolition of crime, although supported by sanctions, abolishes crime.) Their advocacy offered a psychological refuge to those who might otherwise have been overcome by their justifiable fears, but did not offer any realisable solution to the danger.'[4]

We need not at this stage seek to exclude such concepts from the realm of possibility for all time. It is possible that humanity may evolve towards greater virtue, or towards a greater enlightenment about its collective self-interest. Even on such an assumption, however, the question remains: how long will this evolution take before it reaches the point where it can permit the emergence of international institutions of the kind envisaged by a Huizinga or a Toynbee? Past experience suggests that it will be prudent to assume that this process will take a long time. The ancients thought that humanity was getting worse, not better; the Ages of Faith spoke of fallen man, the world as a place of sin, and the realm of virtue a kingdom not of this world. The idea of the betterment of men on earth, progress through education towards a more rational and moral society, is historically recent, and insecurely established. There is no clear evidence that men have behaved better in the few centuries that have passed since the emergence of this idea than they did before. In our time the most famous preacher of the need for 'a change of heart'—Frank Buchman—was also an admirer of Adolf Hitler, under the impact of whose actions many have returned to older ideas of man as incurably sinful and perhaps growing worse. There is no clearer evidence for the 'deterioration' hypothesis than for the more cheerful one. The only diagnosis of man's condition which retains any plausibility is that which the 'electric message' once conveyed about the ailing Victoria: *She is no better, she is much the same.*

The most optimistic assumption reasonably possible is that he may slowly get a little better (more enlightened). That leaves the reign of justice and equity, the virtuous Areopagus of the world, still far in the future. In the meantime what is to become of the interesting bunch of bums that we actually are? Huizinga, writing in 1938, could hardly face this question, or indeed apply his theory of 'play' at that time to international politics, without despair. If he jumps as he does from the 'bad playlessness' which he saw in 1938 to the 'good playlessness' of some indefinite future, it was that the reality of play in his time had assumed so rough a form that it was unbearable for him to contemplate it.

[4] *The Cold War as History*, London, 1967, pp. 176–7.

For his claim that 'play' had disappeared from international life at this time cannot be sustained: what had happened was that 'play' had taken, as it so easily can, a very ugly turn.

At this time the international stage was occupied by the Fascist dictators, who were deliberately using all the technique of stage-craft for their war-dance. Huizinga tries to repel this from 'play' by using the German phrase '*tierischer Ernst*' ('animal seriousness'). Yeats, four years before, had been more perceptive when he spoke of a nation as being 'like an audience in some great theatre . . . watching the sacred drama of its own history' and said that to bring about 'unity of culture' any government or party would need 'force, marching men' and promise 'not this or that measure but a discipline or way of life; that sacred drama must to all native eyes and ears become the greatest of the parables'.[5] The whole dramatic, 'play' side of politics was in 1938 dominated by the Fascist Powers: the Nuremberg Rally and the Nuremberg Ring were theatre, religion and politics all together.

As against this, the democratic politics of the day were deliberately, almost ostentatiously, drab and prosaic. It was these—and not politics generally—that had become 'playless'. The symbolic figure of the League of Nations was its Secretary-General, Sir Eric Drummond, a model of self-effacement in the best public style of the British Civil Service; 'by temperament a man of prudence'.[6] The idea of getting the League of Nations 'into the picture' in the manner of Trygve Lie would have been abhorrent to him: the thought that a senior civil servant, albeit an international one, could think of himself as Lie's successor did, as a naked victim strapped to a sacrificial altar, would have filled him with embarrassment. The traditions of the British Civil Service are admirable but anti-dramatic; drama, ceremonial and symbolism are after all adequately supplied by other parts of the British system of government, as Bagehot saw. But in the League of Nations there was nothing to compensate for an anti-dramatic Secretariat, nothing to combat what Bernanos called *le chômage du cœur*, the unemployment of the heart. The League had the sense of the *sacred*—even strongly developed—but in a low-church mode, repelling ritual and drama. André Maurois compared the Palais de Nations to 'a Protestant place of worship', and developed the comparison:

'Every year during the first week in September a great and sacred orator (such as was the late Père Briand or as is the Reverend Arthur Henderson) preaches before the Assembly of Nations a solemn sermon on a text of the covenant. Then the

---

[5] *Commentary on the three Songs, Poetry*, December 1934.
[6] F. P. Walters, *A History of the League of Nations*, p. 79.

Congregation sings its favourite psalms: Psalm 159, Disarmament. Security; Psalm 163, Security. Disarmament; Psalm 137. Must politics, gentlemen, have precedence over Economics?

'It is an excellent thing for the disbeliever to undergo Church discipline, for ceremonial of any kind lulls to sleep and calms the passions.

'The annual Assembly is more like a religious ceremony than a parliamentary debate; orators unconsciously adopt the tone of the preacher; the word "peace" recurs in every phrase as does in other places of worship the word "God" and it is pronounced in the same way.'[7]

Mr de Traz himself emphasised the undramatic, non-agonistic character of these proceedings: 'An appeal to the passions is not allowed. . . . Collective emotion can have no place. There are no incidents.'

All the play had gone, for the time, out of peace: all 'play' was the acting out of the will to power, 'force, marching men', the Nietzschean dance of joy. In that same year in which Huizinga finished *Homo Ludens*, Yeats wrote *High Talk:*

> *Processions that lack high stilts*
> *have nothing that catches the eye.*

And, in the same year, *Under Ben Bulben:*

> *You that Mitchel's prayer have heard,*
> *'Send war in our time, O Lord! . . .'*

Followers of Ingmar Bergman will remember the serving maid who calls 'God Odin come!' at the beginning of *The Virgin Spring*.

Johan Huizinga died in 1945, the year of the adoption of the Charter of the United Nations. The victorious allies showed themselves conscious, as the pre-war democracies had not been, of the importance of symbolic action, ritual and ceremonial, what Huizinga had meant by 'play'. The wording of the Preamble, and the proceedings in the San Francisco Opera House showed this. So did the complementary proceedings of the Nuremberg Trials. Even the choice of Nuremberg for the scene of the trials (though probably fortuitous) seemed to symbolise the idea that a special new 'sacred drama' was required to exorcise the power of the old one, and must be enacted in the same place. The proceedings at San Francisco and at Nuremberg formed together (though they could not be quite simultaneous) a solemn enactment of a secular Last Judgement. On the right, at San Francisco and London, the kingdom of peace was opened to the elect of the peace-loving nations; on the left, at Nuremberg, the

[7] Introduction to *The Spirit of Geneva* by Robert de Traz, London, 1935.

reprobate, 'like stinking goats', were seen being lowered to damnation. As theatre, it was very simple and very effective; as ritual it derived power from ancient belief, and from humanity's apparently ineradicable wish to punish and to be absolved. Guilt was buried with the captives.

Had Huizinga lived he would have seen, I believe, in the United Nations the return of healthy 'play' to international affairs. He would have seen that, for the preservation of peace among actual unimproved men, the agonistic element remains of the greatest importance, for letting off steam, for saving face, for sanctifying retreat, for purification, and in other ways. It may be thought that the present writer is led by the momentum of his argument to exaggerate the importance of the theatrical in the preservation of the peace. I should like therefore to quote in confirmation of the importance of this element, one of the shrewdest and most experienced of living international negotiators. Mr Arthur Lall, formerly Permanent Representative of India at the United Nations, himself played an important part in the evolution of 'parliamentary diplomacy', especially at that crucial stage when, in 1958, the United States for the first time found itself unable to command a safe two-thirds majority in the General Assembly on a critical issue (Anglo-American landings in Lebanon and Jordan). His own talents, which are remarkable, run in the direction of 'quiet diplomacy', assiduous and exacting work behind the scenes, and his sober endorsement of the value of the theatrical is therefore all the more significant.

In his recent book, *Modern International Negotiations: Principles and Practice*, Mr Lall explains that States seldom have recourse to those bodies 'which in terms of the powers conferred upon them by international treaty could come to clear-cut solutions or could enforce them: the International Court of Justice and the Security Council of the United Nations'. This, he says, is in part due to the reluctance of any state to 'part with its discretion'.[8]

'Moreover,' he continues, 'it could be stated as a psychological axiom in relations among sovereign states, that if X were to be taken from or required of state A in order to arrive at a solution of a dispute or situation with state B, state A would prefer to undertake or accept X if persuaded to do so by its peers (or by superior powers), rather than if obliged to do so as the result of findings of a judicial character in a courtroom. In other words, the public exhortations, the invitations to Washington and Moscow, the wooing by important powers, praise for the acumen and wisdom of its statesmen, appeals in the interest of world harmony, and the spotlight and the publicity of international

[8] *Modern International Negotiation: Principles and Practice*, 1966, p. 103.

conferences, go to make up a much more acceptable political context for action by most governments than a courtroom or than wholly quiet diplomacy.

'It is largely for these background reasons that negotiations through large conferences makes so strong an appeal in our time to most nation states. The large conference, par excellence, is the General Assembly of the United Nations with its 117 member states at the end of 1965. Consequently there has been a steady tendency for international issues concerning world peace, security, and disarmament to be brought to the General Assembly rather than to more restricted forums.'

A reading of the Austrian naturalist Konrad Lorenz's *On Aggression* suggests that the 'psychological axiom' which Mr Lall derives from long and close observation of the behaviour of statesmen and of international conferences, refers to something deeply rooted in nature, and not only in human nature. Mr Lorenz gives examples of what he calls the 'mechanisms evolution has "invented" in order to channel aggression along harmless paths, the role played by ritual in this process. . . .'[9] He cites Sir Julian Huxley's studies of the courtship behaviour of the Great Crested Grebe, notes Huxley's description of the development of purely symbolic ceremonies among these birds, and his use of the term *ritualism* to designate this process. 'In other words,' Lorenz continues, 'he equated the cultural processes leading to the development of human rites with the phylogenetic processes giving rise to such remarkable "ceremonies" in animals.'[10] Lorenz goes on to discuss what he calls 'the great parliament of instincts' and asserts that 'it is particularly the drives that have arisen by ritualisation which are so often called upon, in this parliament, to oppose aggression, to direct it into harmless channels, and to inhibit those of its actions that are injurious to the survival of the species'.[11] He gives the following splendid example of the use of ritual drama in the cause of peace:

'There is, for example, the marvellous appeasement ceremony, generally known as the "dance" of cranes, which, when the symbolism of its behaviour patterns is fully understood, tempts us to translate it into human language. A bird rears up before another one, unfolding its mighty wings, its beak pointing toward the other bird, its eyes fixed piercingly on him, the very image of ominous threatening; so far the appeasement gesture resembles the preparation for attack; but the next moment the bird turns this exhibition of his own fearfulness away from his opponent

[9] *On Aggression*, New York, 1966, p. xiii.
[10] Ibid, p. 58.
[11] Ibid, p. 67.

by a right about turn; and now, still with widely spread wings, he presents to his partner his defenceless occiput, which, in the European crane and many other species, is decorated with a little ruby-red cap. For seconds, the "dancing" bird remains in this position, expressing in easily understood symbolism that his threat of attack is emphatically not directed against his partner but, on the contrary, away from him, against the wicked world outside, implying in this manner the motive of comradely defence. Now the crane turns again towards his friend and repeats this demonstration of his size and strength, only quickly to turn around once more and perform emphatically a fake attack on any substitute object, preferably a nearby crane which is not a friend, or even on a harmless goose or on a piece of wood or stone which he seizes with his beak and throws three or four times into the air. The whole procedure says as clearly as human words, "I am big and threatening, but not toward you—toward the other, the other, the other".'[12]

Reading these words I was reminded of a speech which Commander Noble, representing the United Kingdom, made to the General Assembly one day in November, 1956. Commander Noble's martial demeanour was appropriate to the delivery of an ultimatum. What he said was that Her Majesty's Government 'could not condone the attack by Israel against Egypt'. Her Majesty's Government, he implied—far from having actually participated with Israel in such an attack only a few days before—disapproved of Israel's attack so much that because of this attack it had been obliged to undertake, not certainly an attack of its own, but a peaceful armed expedition to Egyptian territory, an expedition which for some reason the Egyptians had taken it upon themselves to resist by armed force. Because of this misunderstanding, and at the request of the United Nations, Britain was withdrawing a force whose 'motive of comradely defence' (in crane language) had met with such lack of appreciation. Commander Noble did not present to the Assembly 'his defenceless occiput' (which was in any case equipped not with 'a little ruby-red cap' but with a large pink bald patch) and in other matters of detail his particular 'appeasement ceremony' differed from that of the cranes. Instead of mounting 'a fake attack', he invited his partners in the ritual—the members of the General Assembly—to mount a fake attack—in the shape of the United Nations Expeditionary Force—to fake the attainment of the fake objective for which Britain, with France and Israel, had mounted a real attack. Whatever the differences, however, the ceremonies are similar in their basic character. Both seek to preserve, at the same time, the dignity of the actor, and the

[12] *On Aggression*, pp. 174–5.

peace. And both do so by a highly stylised dramatic performance of solemn import: ritual.

The use of ritual for the purpose of what Lorenz (following N. Tinbergen) calls 'redirected activity'—that is the diversion of aggressive impulse into some relatively harmless channel—constitutes the inner meaning of the United Nations sacred drama. Sacred drama, as we know, does not *always* serve such an end. The sacred drama which was to be, for Yeats, 'the greatest of the parables' involved 'force, marching men' and there is no doubts that Yeats at that time (1933-4) had in mind what he knew of the Continental Fascist movements, with which he was in guarded sympathy, intermittently expressed. This obviously was not a drama of 'redirected activity', but of the concentration and legitimation of aggression—the dance of War in Kurt Jooss's *The Green Table*. If the new drama, that of the United Nations, has a radically different significance this is not principally because of its international composition, or of the language of the Charter, or even—at this stage—of the experience of the Second World War, for which the old version of sacred drama formed the prologue. The real significance of the new drama is in the realisation, by now almost instinctive, that the destruction of the human race, through its own devices, is now within the bounds of possibility. This realisation seems to bring into play—also in the Huizinga sense—certain very ancient responses, tending, in Lorenz's terms, to 'inhibit' through 'ritualisation' those aggressive actions 'that are injurious to the survival of the species'. There are cases in which logic and consistency, correct reasoning, on the part of governments of great powers, from two or more sets of incompatible promises, could lead to the Third World War. Since, in that case, the species would be within sight of its logical conclusion, the need for survival points, in certain conditions, to the use of the non-logical, of ritual and fantasy, the dance of the crane and of Commander Noble. The United Nations provides a theatre permanently available—in regular or emergency session—for such solemn, absurd and salutary performances.

As in the case of similar performances by other animals, the ritual inhibition of aggressive actions 'that are injurious to the survival of the species' by no means implies the inhibition of *all* aggression. The United Nations is a gathering of representatives of States—that is to say of persons who have in common (with the usual exception as regards 'China') the fact that they have the confidence, for the time being, of persons who are deemed to have control, for the time being, of the apparatus of coercion and repression in certain named territories. Those governments that can be changed by free and impartially conducted elections constitute a small and dwindling minority of the membership (though it is true that the results of free and impartially conducted elections in the United States can change the foreign policies, and sometimes the governments, of a number of Member nations not otherwise affected by democratic process). Countries with governments liable to be changed by military coup—or by elections conducted within strict limits of military and police tolerance—number at least sixty, more than half the membership. The membership as a whole rests on 'force' in the Sorelian sense, that is to say on the capability of using sanctioned violence in the name of the State, and in the special interests of the minority that controls the apparatus of the State. The methods which gain such control may be very crude—armoured cars to the Palace—or highly sophisticated as in the democratic conventions which ensure peaceful transfers of political power, from one grouping of the middle class—winners in the economic struggle for survival—to another. Or it may be sophisticated in another way, as in the processes of intra-party manœuvres which mysteriously produce the latest heirs of Lenin. But however control over 'force' is won, it cannot be won without 'aggression' in the biological sense; no one of course admits to 'aggression' in the political sense—though many are accused of doing so—and the United Nations has almost given up its long and futile effort to define aggression.

The Members of the United Nations, then, at any given moment in time collectively represent a kind of planetary Burkean 'natural aristocracy' (though one that would have surprised Burke): a power 'growing wild from the rank, productive of the human mind', in the conditions prevailing over the earth's surface (except for China). The Members of the United Nations are all 'peace-loving' in the terms of Chapter II of the Charter—the original Members simply assumed themselves to be so (Articles 3 and 4) and the other Members had to be deemed to be so as a condition of Membership (Article 4). But in order to qualify to be thought of as 'peace-loving', they had in fact to be exceptionally tough and ambitious in terms of their local conditions. Not that the actual people who hold the seats in the Assembly are necessarily exceptional in this way: the Permanent Representative may be the incapable nephew of a great potentate, or the inconvenient rival of a successful democrat. But the nominator must be tough—the potentate great, the democrat successful—or the Permanent Representative will become impermanent. He may not be a success himself but he is, while he lasts, the vicar of the Goddess Success as she manifested herself within certain degrees of latitude and longitude and between certain dates.

Those, then, whose responsibility it is, through the United Nations, to protect Man from the worst consequences of his aggressive impulses are themselves among the most successfully aggressive of mankind. This in itself may be what some social scientists call 'eufunctional'; successful aggressors have a certain understanding of the workings of aggression, and those who have survived to win some important and often dangerous contests have probably on the average a better understanding than most others of what is required for survival. This understanding will not, of course, operate to prevent conflicts which such people think do not seriously threaten their survival, and which may be profitable to them. But they will operate to reduce, as far as they can, the likelihood of that which threatens the survival of all, and can be profitable to none: world wide conflict between the superpowers.

The so-called 'balance of terror', and not the existence of the United Nations, remains the primary guarantee against the outbreak of such a conflict. That guarantee is not, however, so secure and so perfected that humanity can afford to neglect the use of secondary guarantees, giving the primary guarantee, and the instincts which protect the survival of the species, time to do their work. This is the sphere of the United Nations, the ritual at the brink.

The ritual at the brink is also a ritual of the solidarity of the human species, under the threat of nuclear destruction. All the branches of the human race are represented in this ritual; all are here under the same menace. Competing sections of one branch—primarily for the moment the white branch—seek support from the other branches for their competition with the opposing section of their own. Nor is it only a question of competition and opposition. Rituals of nominal hostility covering tacit condonation have high importance in the working of survival, and for such rituals the participation of all the branches, in a dramatised 'verdict of humanity' is essential. Thus those Asian and African States which allowed themselves to be drawn, by various means, into 'condemning' the Soviet Union over Hungary were in appearance handing down a moral verdict; in actual fact they were helping the United States to save its dignity while refraining from intervention. Those Asian and African States which abstained, on the other hand, helped to save the dignity of the Soviet Union, also important in the negotiation of this dangerous corner. Those who were apparently 'on opposite sides' were in fact playing their appropriate parts in a ceremony of survival.

The necessities of such ceremonies, with their demands for the widest possible participation, are also favourable to survival, in the longer term, by producing pressures for inter-racial accommodation. Here white needs black and brown, and must concede something to black and brown: as much as possible in purely nominal terms, but something also in real terms, and probably more as the years go by.

The same interplay which helps to protect the general survival, by rendering the rivalry of the superpowers as harmless as possible, probably also tends in the direction of local conflicts, in certain conditions. More precisely, it tends in the direction of reversing the results of local conflicts, in cases where these have taken the form of white domination over non-white majorities (there is no State in which the converse phenomenon exists). The same interplay which destroyed the Independent State of Katanga—an ill-disguised white-supremacy regime—has now produced economic sanctions against Smith's Rhodesia, and threatens to produce similar and perhaps stronger action against South Africa over South-West Africa. In the process of competition and collusion between the superpowers, and of the inter-racial adjustments necessitated by that process, situations of inter-racial 'force' will tend to elicit international 'violence'. Those who are applying the 'force'—that is to say, those who are holding down and humiliating large racially-defined populations by an apparatus of repression—will find the intrusion of 'violence' through outside pressure both wicked and almost inexplicable, and will find the involvement of the United Nations in such pressure and violence a hideous perversion of the original purpose of the Organisation. The rulers of South Africa and their friends—and that much larger class of those who condemn the practices of the rulers of South Africa, but condemn still more any attempt to interfere with them—reject the idea, with its ominous implications, that South African practice constitutes 'a threat to the peace'. Yet, if the survival of the species requires an acceptance of the basic solidarity of the species as seems probable—the white monopoly of nuclear weapons is already broken—then conditions in which one variety of the species oppresses others, by reason of the mere fact that they are different varieties, do constitute a danger to the survival of the species—a threat to the peace in the most basic sense of the term. There is therefore no contradiction, but a profound harmony, between the role of the United Nations in helping to safeguard the survival of the species, and its role in trying to end situations in which one variety of that species, by its treatment of others, implicitly or explicitly denies the solidarity of the species, and executes that denial by the use of oppressive force. It is the behaviour of the dominant variety, and not the resentment of that behaviour by the other varieties, that constitutes the primary threat to the peace.

There are those who are likely to find the emphasis here placed on race-war excessive, and to insist that class-war, rather than race-war, is primary. This may be so, but the United Nations is not an organisation of primary data; it is an association of sovereign States, organised on a territorial basis, varying widely in their class structure, and accepting the principle (Article 2.7) of non-interference in one another's domestic affairs (except in certain cases where a 'threat to the peace' may arise). The rules of the game tend to exclude specific reference to class-war, and the poor world, in so far as the States that represent it manifest any political solidarity, has tended to identify itself racially (the 'Afro-Asian bloc'). The poor countries, as such, have acted together only on specifically economic questions, uniting to demand higher prices for basic commodities, etc; as this demand has not been backed by combined action on other issues it remains largely unheeded. It is true that revolutionary movements in the underdeveloped world can count on some degree of help from Russia and/or China (just as counter-revolutionary movements can count on help, on a larger scale, from the United States). But the acceptance of Czech or Chinese rifles, etc., does not necessarily imply political solidarity—whatever friend or foe may hope or fear—as is proved by the recent history of Egypt and Syria and Algeria, and of China itself. Nor are there definite signs of a general development of alternative means combining the action of the non-possessing across international lines, *except* in so far as the non-possessing may be identified racially. Certainly the ceremonies of the United Nations, which formalise realities of international relations, take little or no direct account of the class-struggle. The class-balance inside a Member nation will shift from time to time—violently or otherwise—and the international posture of that Member will shift also, to a minor or major extent, and with it its voting pattern, and significance in the United Nations. But, within the universally accepted conventions—formalised in Article 2.7 of the Charter—this change, in itself, cannot be an acknowledged concern of other Members. If the change is of importance, one group will accuse another of having instigated it by 'indirect aggression' or 'imperialist conspiracy' as the case may be. But nobody openly upholds the principle of waging class-war across international boundaries, the principle, that is, of the *Internationale*, of worldwide class-war. At the United Nations there is no stauncher upholder of the 'principle of national sovereignty' than the Soviet Union. The ceremonies are conducted, not in terms of overt class conflict, but in terms of territorial units, and of associations of these units which have come about on an historical and geographical basis (western Europe) as a result of military and political events (Soviet bloc), of economic domination (Western hemisphere), or a sense of community produced by inter-racial experiences (Afro-Asian group/African group). These groupings have varying degrees of solidity, but all have shown enough stability to indicate that they are based on real interests, however established. And it is the interplay of these interests, around the common interest in survival, that constitutes the life of the United Nations.

In the belief that the life of the United Nations may be a necessary part of the continuance of human life generally, I should like to plead for a greater concentration of intelligent interest on the United Nations as it actually is. At present, most interpretative writing on international affairs can be divided into the following categories, as far as the United Nations is concerned:

1. A small number of serious, comprehensive studies by academic specialists on international affairs. The best such study known to me is Professor Inis L. Claude's *Swords into Plowshares*.

2. Writings by Quakers and other students connected with the peace movement—e.g. Messrs Sydney Bailey and Elmore Jackson—concerned with the question of how the Organisation may be improved.

3. Writing designed to elicit favourable feelings about the United Nations as it is. Such writing usually omits such United Nations 'facts of life' as the predominant influence of the United States and the way in which that influence has been used. Those who have accepted such flattering pictures of the United Nations naturally tend to become disgusted with 'the Organisation' when they begin to discover some of its realities. There was an abundance of such writing, mainly in the United States, in the early days; there is less now.

4. Writing designed to disparage the existing United Nations, by comparison with an ideal organisation of a millenary or Platonic nature (Toynbee, etc.).

5. Attacks on the United Nations. Most of these are from the far right, and mostly influenced by the assumption that the United Nations is, or is about to become, a world government. This class of writing combines several of the illusions of classes 3 and 4 with a hysterically xenophobe emotional content. In the 'attacks' category also may be included Chinese and Chinese-inspired polemics and Soviet polemics of certain periods (e.g. 1960–1).

6. Philippisings; ostensibly analytic or descriptive writings designed to serve the interests of a particular State.

7. Realistic writing about power politics, leaving the United Nations almost entirely out of account, and implying that it has no purchase on reality. Louis J. Halle's otherwise impressive *The Cold War* belongs in this category.

8. Writings preoccupied with the measurement of whatever in the United Nations can be measured, often without much concern as to any conceivable use to which such data might be put. This is a relatively recent category, of which probably the most notable example is the Alker-Russett study, *World Politics in the General Assembly*, referred to earlier in this book.

9. More or less detailed and specialised studies, dealing for example with some particular issue before the United Nations (e.g. Algeria), or the United Nations from the standpoint of some particular nation (e.g. Goodwin's *Britain and the United Nations*).

10. Reflections of people with United Nations experience. These can be broken down into sub-categories:

> (a) Contributions to theory. The most notable example is Mr Arthur Lall's *Modern International Negotiations*,
> (b) Memoirs including reflections on experience (those of Trygve Lie, General Von Horn, Mr Tavares de Sá, the present writer). Certain passages in Hammarskjold's *Markings* are related obliquely to this category.

11. Semi-official writings, both signed and unsigned, by serving officials of the Secretariat; approved by their superiors in accordance with Staff Regulations; often in rebuttal of writings in category 10(b).

12. Commentaries by journalists accredited to the United Nations. Some of these (for example Mr Andrew Boyd of the *Economist*, Mr Eric Britter of *The Times*, Mr William Fulton of the *Chicago Tribune*) know the United Nations extremely well, and their comments—as well as their factual reports—are important and useful. There are, however, two limiting factors: one is that imposed (in varying degrees) by newspaper policy in the selection of material used; the second, more important, is inherent in the necessary concern of a practicing journalist not to cause sources to 'dry up' either by 'indiscreet' revelation or by excessively candid comment.

With the exception of categories three to six, all these contain useful material and the first category contains at least one indispensable work. Yet in proportion to what the United Nations represents, this constitutes as a whole a rather disappointing body of literature. One senses, among the more serious-minded and 'hard' students of international affairs a disposition to believe that world peace is really preserved by the 'balance of terror' and by that alone, that it may be best strengthened by sophisticating retaliation techniques and thereby increasing their 'credibility', and that the United Nations is little more than a device for calming the nerves of middle-aged ladies.

I should like to plead for a re-examination of this opinion and for a new concentration of attention—not by specialists in international affairs alone—on the existing United Nations, with a view, not to an impossible perfection, but to increasing as far as we can the effectiveness of what we have now.

The 'balance of terror', which is indeed the primary safeguard of peace, is not a reason for ignoring the United Nations, but for studying it more attentively, since the United Nations both expresses the balance of terror and helps to give it time, room and means to work. The cerebrations of the nuclear games-theorists, and their assumptions about the counter-cerebrations of their 'opposite numbers', are not so sure a shield that we can afford to neglect instinctive and emotional factors, the saving possibilities of myth, ritual and drama.

This book seeks to point in the direction of some of these possibilities. It also seeks to show how the United Nations might gain, or regain, more of the sacred authority which it requires to have in reserve for the fulfilment of its ritual task of emergency mediation. To this end it makes the following recommendations, all of which requires changes in 'established practice' only:

1. The separation of what are here called the 'spiritual' and the 'temporal' aspects, by:

   (a) Removing responsibility for the execution of local 'peace-keeping operations from the shoulders of the Secretary-General (pp. 134–9 and 222–32) and
   (b) Making such operations self-financing, instead of falling (in whole or part) on the regular budget of the United Nations (pp. 241–3). A distinction might be made between operations decided by the Security Council (to be regarded as underwritten by the permanent members for at least a fixed period from the date of the original decision), and operations recommended by the General Assembly (to be sustained by those supporting the Assembly resolution).

2. The restoration of the moral authority of the Security Council by seating the representatives of the Government which rules in Peking in China's seat without conditions. (Any conditions—such as required agreement to the admission of Formosa as a member—would simply be a new 'gimmick' for keeping out China.)

3. The restoration of the genuinely international character of the Secretariat, by the ending of such practices as the 'bypassing' or 'snowing under' of Soviet—and eventually Chinese—staff members, and the discarding of the invidious assumption that citizens of certain States are really fitted to be international civil servants while others are not. It should be assumed that *all* Staff members who are citizens of major powers will keep in touch with their governments and keep them informed on all important matters coming within their knowledge, and this should not be regarded as a breach of discretion. In local peace-keeping operations, where the conduct of these had aroused the displeasure of certain States, the 'Co-ordinator' (pp. 226–9) or his equivalent would no doubt refrain from placing staff-members who are citizens of these States in positions where they would acquire information which might help these States in undermining the operation in question. This, however, would not affect the position of citizens of these States within the Secretariat proper, or in relation to other peace-keeping operations.

Changes of this order do not require Charter revision, or encroachments on national sovereignty; on the contrary they are closer to the spirit of the Charter, as originally understood, and more respectful of national sovereignty, than is existing practice. It is true, however, that such changes, if made, would represent concessions—or at least the yielding of certain apparent short-term advantages—on the part of that Power which has done most to shape the status quo. This is obvious in the case of the second recommendation (China) and of the third (Russian and Chinese staff members); it also applies to the first recommendation, since this Power has derived advantages from the temporal involvements of the Secretary-General (Lie in Korea, Hammarskjold in the Congo) and from accepted methods of peace-keeping.

None of these advantages, however, represents a vital interest of the Power concerned. The strengthening of the moral authority of the United Nations, as an emergency reserve for use in the preservation of world peace, *is* a vital interest of that Power, as of every other. There are therefore grounds to hope that that Power—without whose assent no early major changes in practice could be brought about—may come to consider changes of this character to be in conformity with its long-term national interest.

But before things can begin to move in this direction, there must be a quickening of interest in the United Nations as it actually functions. Such a quickening must affect opinion in the English-speaking world to begin with, both because it is there that there has been the most continuous and hopeful interest in the United Nations, and because of the predominant position of the United States. If a 'United Nations revival' in the English-speaking world were founded on a serious appreciation of the actual possibilities of 'the Organisation' and on a recognition of a common human interest in—for example—reducing philippising to a minimum, one may feel reasonably sure that after an initial phase of suspicion, such a revival would begin to strike a responsive note in Eastern Europe and the Soviet Union. Once it did so, the quickening of interest would soon be world-wide.

The farther we seem from such a revival—and we seem far indeed at present—the more urgent it is to set about establishing the conditions for it. The process must begin, I believe, among those who are already internationally minded—in the peace movement, inside the United Nations Secretariat, among the members of Delegations, in the United Nations Associations and similar bodies—and even inside the State Department, under the protecting sign of the Credibility of Our Image. It should begin with conscious acts of rejection: a refusal to idealise the existing United Nations, and a refusal to set up in its stead an imaginary Organisation suited to a regenerate mankind. This should be followed by a concentration of realistic and explicit interest on the existing United Nations. The explicitness is as important as the realism: at present the number of those who understand the reality of United States predominance in the United Nations greatly exceeds the number of those who discuss this phenomenon with any freedom. There even exist depressing little books, written in idealistic language for the instruction of the young, which are designed to conceal this fact of international life.

Informed internationalists, and the peace-movement generally, should become less tolerant of such cant, and more insistent on knowing, and speaking clearly about, international realities at the United Nations. In that way also the young would be likely to become more interested in a United Nations which would be an intelligible part of the real and dangerous world in which they hope to live. They are not at all interested in the paralytic and bankrupt Santa Claus which some well-meaning and some other persons at present offer as the focus of their international aspirations.

It may be considered that this emphasis on realism in the *study* of the United Nations is at variance with my emphasis on myth and ritual in the *working* of 'the Organisation'. If the workings are better understood, will not the myth and ritual lose their power? Philosophically, the objection is well-founded, and in part factually also: the ritual use made of the United Nations at the time, for example, of the Suez-Hungary double crisis depended for its effectiveness on a large measure of public illusion and confusion (pp. 276–9, etc.) If the area of illusion and confusion—Burke's 'decent drapery'—is sensibly curtailed, will not the danger in future emergencies be increased?

To this serious objection the following points make up, I believe, an adequate reply:

First, the danger at present is not from a diminution of illusion and confusion but from a growing indifference—stemming in part from illusion, confusion and the past exploitations of these —towards the United Nations, resulting in a diminution of its moral authority, and hence in the diminished power of its ritual. It is true that this is only an 'interim' answer, but then it is through a series of 'interims' that we have to live, with the current one always the most urgent.

Second, there are different levels of public opinion: there are those who give more or less serious and continuous thought to international relations, and those who only fitfully, and in the main during major crises, attempt to form some concept of 'what is going on'. People in the second category, which is much the larger, *necessarily* see each international crisis in terms of some kind of myth, and will be only faintly and indirectly affected by the results of any realistic studies. This is a regrettably 'elitist' argument but the world at present—our 'interim' world—is a regrettably elitist place. Even Chairman Mao, in his *Talks to the Yenan Forum*, conceded that the literature suited to the masses was not the literature required by the cadres.

Third, religious, political and scientific thought proceeds by the construction of myths—hypotheses at a later stage—and by the critique of these myths. The more powerful, vivid, and important the myth the greater the need for the critique. The myth itself has always comprised within it the need and the duty to ask questions about it. The Grail Legend, for example, insists on the disastrous consequences that follow if the right questions are not asked:

'A great sorrow has recently been brought on the land by a young knight who was welcomed as a guest by the rich Fisher King. To him appeared the Holy Grail and the lance with angry blood welling from its point. He did not ask whom it served or whence it came and because he did not ask this, all the lands are stirred up to war and no knight meets another in the forest without striking him down and killing him if he can.'[13]

Realistic study does not, then, imply any present danger to the power of myth and ritual in international relations; it may lead to a better understanding of how these work and how they may more effectively be used to safeguard peace and may thereby

---

[13] Quoted in Jessie Weston, *From Ritual to Romance*.

conduce to the survival of our species into better times in which such devices may have come to seem crude and archaic.

If this transit is to be achieved there is an urgent need not only for a more realistic and exacting interest in United Nations studies among members of the peace movement but also for a concentration of scholarly and other expert interest, from many disciplines and fields of activity, into such studies. A combined enquiry which might test, among other things, the validity of the ideas here put forward—might have the following as its terms of reference:

To recommend means whereby the United Nations, under its present Charter, and without encroachment on national sovereignty, might be developed in such a way as to provide the maximum safeguards for human survival, now and over the next ten years (the study to be renewed before the end of that period).

Participants in such a study might be drawn from among the following:

i. People with experience of important phases of United Nations activity—in Security Council, General Assembly or Secretariat—but no longer in the service of the United Nations or of a Member State;

ii. journalists with long experience of the daily workings of the United Nations;

iii. specialists in international affairs (other than those experts whose work consists in propagating myths desired by national governments, or in obfuscation for its own sake);

iv. political scientists who are not specialists in international affairs and who are somewhat suspicious about those who are;

v. anthropologists, particularly those with a special interest in conflict resolution;

vi. zoologists interested in redirected activity (like Konrad Lorenz);

vii. psychologists;

viii. scholars whose interest in language connects with the study of social change through new uses of language (I. A. Richards, Kenneth Burke, Noam Chomsky);

ix. lawyers with a similar range of interest;

x. scientists, irrespective of their field, who are personally deeply concerned about the problem of peace, as Freud and Einstein were;

xi. others, including specialists in communication and propaganda; admen who want to save their souls, etc.;

xii. priests, perhaps;

xiii. poets, sometimes;

xiv. Quakers, still.

The 'disciplines' participating in such a study would be much less important than the people. For the study to produce anything useful the participants would have to be imbued with the conviction that human survival is in fact in danger and is more important than any national, sectional or ideological interest. They would have to understand what 'philippising' is, not to be discouraged by its prevalence, and to refrain most strictly from indulging in it themselves. The underwriting of such a study is of course less easy than the underwriting of the more genteel forms of philippising, but it is perhaps not impossible.

I hope that anyone who has read these pages and who feels —whatever disagreement there may be about even the larger details—that there may be some merit in the general thesis and that a systematic non-philippising study with this as a starting-point would be worth while, will communicate with the author. From such communications and from discussions based on them might come the beginnings of a sustained and multiple enquiry, accompanying the working of the United Nations over the years. The sacred drama has instinct already on its side, in the shape of the will to survive, and this is much; but, for greater security, instinct needs to be supplemented by criticism, it needs not just the *claque* which now sustains this or that performer, but a multiplicity of variously endowed critics, not only in order that the audience, or parts of it, may understand a little better but also so that the performers themselves may better understand their roles, their partners and their audience.

No such multiple criticism in depth now exists. This book is not an example of such criticism—which when it comes must combine many kinds of insight, and the resources of a number of minds and discipline—but an attempt to demonstrate that the proceedings on the East River deserve and require exacting and sustained attention if the safeguards of survival are not to be lowered.

In our time such great men as Freud and Einstein have devoted much of their concern, and some part of their attention, to the problem of preventing war. The results of their ponderings are curiously disappointing. Freud, questioned by Einstein on the subject, replied in terms of generalities about individual and family psychology, the death wish and so on.[14] Einstein himself, in the years after the Second World War, spoke and wrote repeatedly on the subject, and the authority of his name, combining with the strength of his convictions and the inadequacy of his information, left the subject even more befogged than it had been before. Einstein was, of course, a 'world government' man, and correspondingly dissatisfied with the United Nations which

[14] *Character and Culture*, Chapter X, 'On War'.

none the less he recognised as 'the only instrument we have to work with in our struggle to achieve something better'[15] (1946). This was reasonable enough: it was around the methods by which 'something better' could be attained that confusion set in. 'In the future,' said Einstein in a 1947 broadcast, 'the legislative assembly of the United Nations must be composed of men and women who are responsible not to national governments but only to the people who elect them.'[16] To this Assembly the Security Council would be subordinated and the 'Veto' thereby eliminated. World government would be instituted on this basis. Later in the same year he developed these ideas in an 'Open Letter to the General Assembly'.[17] He now considered the possibility that the Government of the Soviet Union might refuse to join the sovereign democratic General Assembly. If so, he thought, there could be set up a 'partial world government which would have to be very strong . . . comprising at least two thirds of the major industrial and economic areas of the world'.[18] This 'partial world government' must, however, never 'act as an alliance against the rest of the world'[19]. How it was to be prevented from evolving in that direction he did not say.

It is hardly surprising that the trend of these reflections provoked alarm in the Soviet Union. Four Soviet scientists undertook to reply. They described the world government idea as 'nothing but a flamboyant signboard for the world supremacy of the capitalist monopolies'.[20] The idea of a popularly elected sovereign General Assembly was 'a political fad which plays into the hands of the sworn enemies of sincere international co-operation and enduring peace'. They also pointed out, quite correctly at that time, that the existing General Assembly was dominated and controlled by the United States.

Einstein's reply was gentle and patient in tone—and the letter of the Soviet scientists had shown proper respect to him personally—but it clearly implied that he thought the Soviet scientists had been brainwashed. Arguments to the effect that the Assembly was controlled by the United States impressed him, he said, as 'a kind of mythology; they are not convincing'.[21]

In retrospect it is clear that Einstein himself had been brainwashed by the 'mythology' of the American press of the period; the thought that such a brain can be thus washed is in itself alarming. It would hardly be contested today, even by the most

[15] *Einstein on Peace*, edited by O. Nathan and H. Norden. London, 1963; p. 386.
[16] Ibid, p. 416.
[17] Ibid, p. 440.
[18] Ibid.
[19] Ibid.
[20] Ibid, p. 445. The reply was published in *New Times*, 26 November 1947.
[21] Ibid.

faithful philippiser in Philip's employment, that the United States did control an absolutely safe two-thirds majority in the General Assembly at the time of Einstein's reply (December 1947) and over the first ten years of the organisation's existence. Nor would world-wide popular elections—to the small extent that these might have been attainable—have given a significantly different result. The minority of countries which had working national systems of political democracy already in practice 'elected' their delegates, although indirectly. The non-democracies would not permit genuine elections—producing in effect the nucleus of an alternative, more 'legitimate' national government —unless they were forced to do so. By whom?

It is clear that Einstein here simply did not know the data about which he believed himself to be reasoning. Unfortunately his prestige has encouraged scientists after him to think in terms of what ought to replace the United Nations—for that is what 'reform' of the order imagined by Einstein would mean—rather than of how the United Nations actually works. Thus the otherwise valuable *Bulletin of the Atomic Scientists*,[22] although devoted to the same object as the United Nations—the object of the Preamble—has given remarkably little attention to what actually happens on the East River. Similarly the results of a recent gathering of behavioural scientists,[23] examining the question of the prevention of international conflict, gave only the most perfunctory and peripheral recognition to the fact that there does exist a large, expensive and active international institution set up by the governments of the world to try to achieve the purpose with the possibilities of whose attainment the scientists were concerned.

In the sacred drama by the East River, the realities and fantasies of international life mingle, collide and take new shapes from interaction. The process ought surely to attract more serious interest than it has so far done. The predominance of the fantastic, which has tended to repel the serious student, ought on the contrary to attract his concentrated attention. Sacred drama can be a preparation for war, as with *Cathleen ni Houlihan* or the Nuremberg Rallies; or a substitute for it, as it has often been at the United Nations—on Suez and Hungary in 1956, for example; or it can be dangerously ambiguous, a substitute so intensely felt as to merge somnambulistically into a disastrous reality, as did the passionate performances of

---

[22] In *The Atomic Age. Articles from the Bulletin of the Atomic Scientists: 1945-62*, the only references indexed to the United Nations are to specialised agencies and the Radiation Committee. Yet the Bulletin is not a publication for specialists and is primarily concerned with the preservation of peace.

[23] *International Conflict and Behavioural Science: The Craigville Papers*, Edited by Roger Fisher. New York, 1964.

President Nasser. We need to know much more about how the forces actually work that have proved so destructive and so salutary. It is in the theatre of the East River—and the clinical associations of 'theatre' are not out of place either—that they can be studied.

Considering what this institution was founded to do, in the words of the Preamble, and considering that it has survived for more than two decades and has not altogether failed, it is surely time that more minds, and more of the best minds, were preoccupied with its nature and its future. He who is capable of such enquiry and refrains from it—through impatience, indifference, or contempt—might think of himself as perhaps repeating the essence of that earlier ominous failure in holy curiosity:

> 'He did not ask whom it served or whence it came and because he did not ask this, all the lands are stirred up to war. . . .'

APPENDIX:

THE LEOPARD-SKIN PRIEST
David Brokensha
Department of Anthropology, University of California, Santa Barbara

THIS APPENDIX consists of anthropological comments on certain of the main themes, considered in relation to traditional methods of conflict resolution in selected African societies. I choose my examples from Africa partly because of the importance of African nations in the United Nations, as mentioned several times; also, my anthropological enquiries have been conducted mainly in African societies. And as the author points out, 'The Africans, perhaps because their own politics contain such large elements of symbolism and drama, seem to have grasped from the beginning the true possibilities of the United Nations'.

Modern anthropological studies of methods of settling disputes in economically simple societies reveal a state vastly different from that envisioned by Hobbes, who saw 'the condition of a man—[as] a condition of war of everyone against everyone ... [where all have a] continual fear and danger of violent death'. (*Leviathan*, Pt. I, Ch. 4 and Ch. 13.) Details of contemporary studies of conflict resolution will be found in the works cited in the Bibliography. (See especially Bohannan, 1967; Gluckman, 1956; Nader, 1965.) Topics that engage the attention of anthropologists include a consideration of the difference between societies with highly organised centralised political systems, and stateless societies, lacking formal courts or political leaders: examples will be presented from both types of society. Distinctions are also made between conflicts at different levels, the main difference being those within and those beyond the range of domestic kinship. The difference is explicitly recognised by participants: among the Nuer, Dinka, Lugbara and Suku, for example, fights between members of the same lineage are conducted with clubs or with bare hands, whereas spears are used for 'strangers'. If a war occurs between members of the same Nuer tribal section, no houses are destroyed, nor are women or children injured, nor are captives taken, all of which are permissible in a wider-scale war. In any event, such wars seldom involved many casualties, for a variety of economic, logistic and moral reasons.

Finally, the anthropologists have stressed, with varying degrees of emphasis, the central importance of reconciliation. Particularly where the disputants have close ties, the main aim in resolving conflict is to restore amity, to rebuild good relationships, rather than to punish the offender. As Bohannan remarked of the Tiv of Northern Nigeria, 'Truth in Tivland is an elusive matter because smooth social relationships are deemed of higher cultural value than mere precision of fact'. It follows that the aim is not to establish 'facts' and to reach a clear-cut decision, as courts attempt to do, but to effect an acceptable compromise.

I shall examine mechanisms of conflict resolution from four African societies, the Nuer of the Southern Sudan, the Arusha of northern Tanzania, the Larterians of southern Ghana, and the Swazi of southern Africa. The first two societies represent different degrees of 'statelessness, while the others have well-developed political organisations.

a THE NUER (*Evans-Pritchard, 1940 and 1956*)

Ritual authority is found in many societies: among the Konkomba of northern Ghana, for example, 'the Elders' authority is moral and ritual . . . though he has no power to punish by force, to run counter to his commands is itself sacrilege'. (David Tait, in Middleton and Tait, 1958, p. 199.) And the Dinka of southern Sudan recognise the 'masters of the fishing-spear', leaders who mediate the divine to men, and who form a dual association with the warriors. (Godfrey Lienhardt, in Middleton and Tait, 1958, pp. 118–31.) One of the best analyses of such ritual authorities is that made by Professor E. E. Evans-Pritchard of the leopard-skin priests of the Nuer.

The Nuer, a pastoral people who live in the wide savanna plains of the southern Sudan, have a minimum of government. 'The Nuer constitution is highly individualistic and libertarian. It is an acephalous state, lacking legislative, judicial and executive organs. Nevertheless it is far from chaotic. It has a persistent and coherent form of what might be called "ordered anarchy". The absence of centralised government and bureaucracy in the nation, the tribe and in tribal segments . . . is less remarkable than the absence of any persons who represent the unity and exclusiveness of these groups.' In this segmentary political system, there were no political officers as such; the lineage system was of major importance in providing order. Certain people, however, had moral and religious authority, and had limited powers to settle disputes.

These were the leopard-skin priests (*kuaar twac*), so called from their leopard-skin which was slung around the right shoulder; in a society where the men wore no clothing, this was a particularly effective badge of office. They were by no means chiefs, although they had political functions deriving from the sacred character of their office. Leopard-skin priests, who usually inherited their office, were believed to have a mystical association with the earth, which made their curses very powerful.

When 'a priest acts as intermediary between men and God, the virtue which gives efficacy to his mediation resides in his office rather than in himself. Consequently, it does not matter what sort of person he is, socially, psychologically, or morally.' He is not afforded any elaborate courtesies, for 'priestly duties are tiresome and ill-rewarded, but somebody has to perform them'. This is in accordance with the pragmatic quality of the Nuer life, one that is found in other stateless societies such as the Tiv.

'The chief services a priest performs are in connection with homicide, and the importance of his office derives from this essential function.' The priest is the only one who can perform the ritual duties, which include

i. releasing the killer from his state of ritual danger;

ii. providing sanctuary to the killer, if a blood-feud appears imminent;

iii. negotiating a settlement, which includes settling compensation and pacifying the ghost of the slain man;

iv. performing appropriate sacrifices so that normal social relationships may be resumed;

v. purifying and rehabilitating the killer, to rid him of his blood-guilt. This is treated explicitly as a rite of passage from one state to another, and includes the shaving of the head.

A priest may intervene between opposing factions, and cut a line with a hoe, forbidding either side to cross the line. In this, as in his other activities, he relies on the moral and sacred authority of his office to resolve the conflict. He can be effective only when there is a desire for peace—'his role in disputes may be regarded as a means by which neighbours, who wish a difficulty settled without resource to force and who acknowledge that the other side have a good case, can negotiate'. If the people are unduly obstinate in refusing the priest's mediation, then he can rub ashes on the back of an ox, a sign that he is preparing to slaughter it. Then the dead man's kinsmen, who have been refusing a settlement, should rush to prevent the slaughter saying 'No. Do not kill your ox. It is finished. We will accept compensation.' The point is that all parties know that settlement will be reached, and act out, in this expressive manner, their way to reaching accord.

b. THE ARUSHA (*Gulliver*, 1963)

The Arusha are a group of agricultural Masai who also had in their indigenous society, 'no established and specialised judicial system'. Although courts have since been imposed by outside authorities, traditional procedures for dealing with breaches of norms continue to be used.

First, public assemblies can deal with virtually any kind of dispute 'in an attempt either to obtain a settlement outright, or to further the treatment of the matter towards that end'. By contrast to the Nuer, and other non-centralised societies, there is 'little legitimate opportunity for aggrieved individuals and their supporters to resort to physical violence as self-help'. Gulliver suggests that peaceful discussion as a way of settling disputes is emphasised in order to counter the potential violence of the young warriors; these are given no responsibility in society, in favour of the elders. (This offers an interesting contrast to many contemporary societies which have reversed traditional generational roles, the young being now anxious for peace, while many of their elders favour violence.)

These assemblies (or *moots*) are conducted with great informality. 'Nevertheless, such pragmatic flexibility does not invalidate an orderly attempt at reaching a settlement. There are general principles of proper behaviour underlying all these assemblies . . . The process of establishing a settlement consists of discussion and negotiating, argument and counter-argument, offer and counter-offer', in an attempt to reach a mutually acceptable compromise. In the talks, 'flexibility is a major virtue' and even though participants may not achieve all they had desired, by accepting the proposed compromise they earn popular approval, and show that they are aware of and support correct behaviour.

Gulliver examines differences in disputes between related persons, and those between unrelated persons. 'When the disputants have been in some mutually valuable relationship, then they both have an interest in maintaining or restoring it.' But if no relationship exists, then 'the bargaining power of each against the other is both weaker and of a different order'.

The Arusha are well aware that once a settlement has been reached, there is still the practical difficulty of enforcing it. Where possible, the agreement is put into effect before the assembly disperses: for example, a boundary between fields will be demarcated there and then, or a cow handed over on the spot, to eliminate any possibility of prevarication. Where immediate settlement is physically impossible, the assembly may decide to re-convene in a few days' time expressly for the purpose of witnessing implementation of the agreement. When the dispute is over, mutual agreement is symbolised by each disputant providing beer for all, or perhaps a feast of meat as well. 'Arusha are not naïve enough to think that the mere act of drinking together provides friendly relations . . . [but that] men who drink together tacitly declare their lack of particular enmity and conflict.' Should there be difficulties in implementing the decision, additional means of coercion may be used. These include the delaying of consideration of further disputes until the one in question is settled; the use of physical coercion, and the imposition of penalties; curses and ritual oaths may also be used. These additional means will not be examined in detail; it is sufficient to note that there is a variety of resources, physical and supernatural, available to the Arusha in helping them settle their disputes.

c. THE PEOPLE OF LARTEH (*Brokensha*, 1966)

In contrast to the Nuer and the Arusha, Larteh (a rural town of southern Ghana) is part of a centralised political system, with established courts, and a vast array of political offices. In addition to the regular legal procedures, there are certain extra-judicial methods of solving disputes, two of which will be considered.

'*Begging*.' When a Larterian has offended someone by a breach of one of the norms, he may adopt a device that ensures a quick hearing, and forgiveness, or at most some light punishment. 'Begging' has several aspects: it is an admission of guilt, a public act of contrition, a resolve not to offend in the same way again, and a plea for mercy. The plea is accompanied by the supplicant tapping the back of the right hand in the palm of his left hand, as a gesture of asking for pardon. The supplicant also presents a gift, often a bottle of schnapps or rum, to the person offended; part of the liquor is poured as a libation, the balance drunk by all present. This marks the reconciliation and the restoration of amity.

'Begging' is particularly appropriate when the offence is the result of some thoughtless action, for it provides a formula for a settlement which allows all parties to keep their dignity. For by 'begging', by humbling himself and confessing, the offender gains in moral strength: the onus is then on the person offended to be gracious and forgiving; not to forgive shifts public sympathy away from the person offended, to the offender. 'He tried,' people would say, 'but X was proud and stubborn and would not listen. What else could he do?'

A very similar custom is reported from an Indian community on a Guianese sugar plantation: 'to "give complain" before taking any action is the proper procedure; the suspected offender is thus given the opportunity of assuring the offended person of his good intentions or explaining the reprehensible act in a satisfactory manner. He apologises or performs an act of restitution which restores the relationship to its *status quo* . . . This is called "giving satisfaction" . . . the procedure of "complain" and "satisfaction" is a mechanism for resolving a dispute and protecting the prestige of the contenders at the same time.' (Jayawardena, 1963, p. 80.)

Oaths. By swearing certain forbidden words, often associated with national disasters, any person can swiftly ensure that his grievance will be heard without delay by a court. One of the best known oaths is that of *Wukuda and Sokodei*, referring to a Wednesday, about two centuries ago, when Larteh and associated towns suffered a calamitous defeat at a place called Sokodei. The swearing of the words is thought to release malevolent forces which threaten the welfare of all: it is then necessary to convene a court at once, hear the complaint, establish guilt and impose a fine, part of which is used for the ritual sacrifice of sheep to restore the harmony. For example a man, convinced of his wife's adultery, might lack evidence to sue for damages. He could confront the suspected adulterer and say, 'By Wukuda and Sokodei, you have been fornicating with my wife'. Such a charge is always made before witnesses, who immediately arrest both parties as 'oath-prisoners', and take them to the court. Such a procedure is risky, for the oath-swearer may gain nothing, but it does provide an opportunity for public airing of a grievance, and for rapid settlement.

The mechanisms of 'begging' and of 'oaths' are widely distributed in West African societies: Larteh is chosen as an example simply for convenience. Other recorded methods of resolving conflict include song-duels, oracles, peace-pipes, go-betweens and countless others. The few examples described above illustrate how societies provide procedures to help them settle and contain quarrels: the Nuer use the sacred office of their leopard-skin priests to allow them to reach a settlement with dignity; the Arusha strongly emphasise the virtue of talking it out until a compromise is reached; Larterians have evolved ways of providing opportunity for an apology for a rash act and of expediting a hearing.

d. THE SWAZI (*Gluckman*, 1963)

My last example is taken from Hilda Kuper's account of Swazi royal ritual, as analysed by Max Gluckman. The traditional Swazi annual *incwala* ceremony was held partly to celebrate the first-fruits, but was also a ritual expression of conflict and its resolution. A series of ceremonies centred around the King, who entered the cattle-kraal naked, while the people chanted songs of hate and rejection, the words and the tune being 'wild and sad'. The King several times emerged from a special sanctuary, then retreated into it again, until at last he acceded to the pleadings of his people to come out, and was led out by a group of ritually pure youths. The ceremonies concluded with 'feasting and revelry at the expense of the rulers, and gay love-making'.

Gluckman shows that the ceremonies are an 'acting out of

tensions which make up the national life'. Conflicts are expressly presented at different levels—of king and state against the people; king and commoners against princes; men against nature; the state against internal and external foes. After some reversals of roles, the rites end with a 'cathartic purging'. 'The dramatic symbolic acting of social relations in their ambivalence is believed to achieve unity and prosperity.' This ritual is, of course, of a different order to the others as it is concerned with latent rather than with specific conflicts.

I have briefly described ritual ways of conflict resolution from four African societies. Countless other examples could have been given, but these should suffice to indicate the prevalence of *symbolic elements* in all societies. Although the mechanisms vary greatly, they are all effective, in their expressive ways, of achieving unity.

Finally, I examine some underlying aspects of conflicts in African societies, particularly the notions of anger, peace and amity.

Anger is seen as mystically dangerous: 'the ultimate cause of sickness is thought to be anger, anger in men's hearts', as the Nyakyusa of Tanzania say. There, a chief may be harmed by the 'breath of men', referring to the murmuring of commoners who are justifiably angry with their chief. (Wilson, 1959, pp. 8–9.) Concomitant with the belief in the harmful nature of anger, is one in the beneficial effect of releasing anger. 'By exposing their ill-feeling in a ritual context to beneficial ritual forces, individuals are purged of rebellious wishes and emotions and willingly conform once more to the public mores.' (Turner, 1965, p. 81.) Not only does the venting of anger 'purge rebellious wishes' but it is also often a therapeutic prelude to a simple compromise being accepted.

Peace and *amity* are held up as desirable goals by ancestors and gods, through their priests and religious leaders, all of whom, in normal circumstances, abhor conflict. Consequently they use their ritual authority to effect reconciliation, to restore the equivalence and amity of social relationships. I stress that the mechanisms can only be effective when the disputants are prepared to consider a settlement, and where they incorporate face-saving *agones*. As Evans-Pritchard said of the leopard-skin priest, 'no discussion can be held unless both parties want the dispute settled and are prepared to compromise and submit to arbitration'. (Evans-Pritchard, 1940, p. 164.) And up to the last moment many disputants are likely to keep up a show of intransigence, of allowing themselves to be persuaded.

Although 'the mechanisms believed in appear to us ridiculous, the underlying principle is one that most people would accept.

It is that individual good health and national prosperity depend ultimately on good social relationships—on amity between kinsmen, and neighbours, and fellow-citizens.' (Wilson, 1959, p. 14.)

Conclusion

'The social process of the feud and threat of feud may seem very distant to us, but in fact it is present on our doorsteps. The application of this analysis to international affairs would overlook many complicating factors: is there a single moral order, for example, as among the Nuer? Can nations allow their members to recognise external conflicting ties of loyalty?' (Gluckman, 1956, p. 23.)

Any direct applications to the United Nation, of the mechanisms described above, is clearly impossible; still, it is tempting to consider the Secretary-General, his business-suit discarded for a leopard-skin, sipping honey-beer with the elders, or the British delegate exclaiming, "By Suez", in order to bring quick action, or the Israelis taking the initiative, and, thereby establishing a moral superiority, by 'begging' their enemies to forgive them, if they have offended.

While having no immediate and practical applicability, the anthropological study of conflict serves to reinforce the plea for a combined enquiry into means by which 'the United Nations might be developed in such a way as to provide the maximum safeguards for human survival'. Although making no romantic attempts to revive obsolete customs, or to create spurious new ones, such studies emphasise the nearly universal importance of myth and ritual and symbolism—in fact, of *sacred drama*. Despite the complexities of contemporary international relationships, there is still a need for symbolic elements in negotiation and in the resolution of conflicts. As Claude Levi-Strauss has pointed out, the simpler societies 'may possess a genius for invention in action that leaves the achievements of civilised peoples far behind'; therefore we can all learn from the rituals of the leopard-skin priest.

POSTSCRIPT TO APPENDIX:

Conor Cruise O'Brien

I. That the kind of dramatised holy mediation of which Mr Brokensha gives African examples is of great antiquity in Europe appears from a passage from the historian Diodorus on the Druids, which is quoted in a lecture by Professor James J. Tierney, 'The Celts and the Classical Authors' in the collection *The Celts* (ed. Joseph Raftery, Cork, 1964):

'And it is not only in the needs of peace but in war also that they carefully obey these men and their song-loving poets, and that is true not only of their friends but also of their enemies. For oftentimes as armies approach each other in line of battle with their swords drawn and their spears raised for the charge, these men come forth between them and stop the conflict, as though they had spellbound some kind of wild animals. Thus, even among the most savage Barbarians anger yields to wisdom and Ares does homage to the Muses.'

II. I am indebted to Professor Owen D. Lattimore for a remarkable example of regulated philippising from Mongolia: 'The Manchus were then (1757) strong enough to take the step that settled the affairs of Outer Mongolia until the Revolution of 1911. They decreed that henceforth the reincarnations of the Javzandamba were to be discovered only in Tibet; moreover, no sons or nephews of ruling princes in Mongolia were to be discovered to be greater or lesser reincarnations' ('Religion and Revolution in Mongolia', a Review article by Owen Lattimore in *Modern Asian Studies* 1, 1 (1967)).

A little earlier the French Monarchy had been accused of acting on similar principles:

De par le Roi, défense a Dieu
De faire miracles en ce lieu.

BIBLIOGRAPHY I

(a) UNITED NATIONS, ETC.

The principal source of published material is in the official records of the United Nations, and notably in the verbatim reports of the Security Council and General Assembly (Plenary Sessions). There is an extensive literature about the United Nations; some of the characteristics of this literature are discussed in the text (pp. 290–1). There follows a list of books—not all of them primarily or directly concerned with the existing United Nations—which were found useful, in one way or another, in the composition of the present work, supplementing the writer's own experience as a Delegate to the General Assembly (1956–61) a member of the Secretariat (May–December 1961) and a Representative of the Secretary-General in the field (Katanga, June–November 1961).

N.B. Those works which reflect experience of the inner workings of the United Nations, in the Security Council, the General Assembly, the Secretariat or otherwise (e.g. in peace-keeping operations) are marked with an asterisk:

*ALEXANDER, General H. T.: *African Tightrope* (London 1965)
As Chief of Staff of the Ghana Army the author was concerned with the critical opening stages of the U.N. Congo Operation, of which he gives a first-hand account.

ALKER, HAYWARD R. JR. and RUSSETT, BRUCE M.: *World Politics in the General Assembly* (New Haven 1965) Discussed in text (pp. 18–19)

ARDREY, ROBERT: *The Territorial Imperative: a Personal Inquiry into the Animal Origins of Property and Nations* (New York and Toronto, 1966)
Owes much to Lorenz (q.v.). Politically, the author's sympathies are with South Africa and also 'frankly on the side of instrusion' in Vietnam. The style is appropriately overbearing, but the bibliography will be useful to those interested in the relations between zoology and diplomacy.

BOYD, ANDREW: *United Nations: Piety, Myth and Truth* (London 1962)
The author knows the United Nations exceptionally well, from having covered it for *The Economist* over many years. The book is strongly recommended as a general introduction; a certain tendency to minimise the 'American' factor, should however be allowed for.

CALVOCORESSI, PETER: *World Order and New States: Problems of Keeping the Peace* (New York 1962)
A useful survey, which might profitably be revised from time to time; the outlines of this range of problems have greatly changed in the five years since publication.

CARTHY, J. D. and EBLING, F. J., Jr., editors, *The Natural History of Aggression*, New York and London, 1964.
Record of a symposium at the Institute of Biology in London. Contributions by Lorenz (q.v.) and others. For the present study, the most interesting contribution is that of the psychiatrist, Anthony Storr, who believes that the space race may be 'serving the function of a ritual conflict between East and West'.

Centre de Recherches et Information Socio-Politiques, Brussels: From 1960 to 1963, the annual *Congo* volumes published by the Centre constitute an extremely valuable collection of documents for the history of the United Nations operations in the Congo.

CLAUDE, INIS L.: *Swords into Plowshares: The Problems and Progress of International Organization* (Third ed. revised: New York 1964: London 1965)
Outstandingly the most relevant, perceptive and generally useful of all the academic works about the United Nations known to the present writer.

*CLEVELAND, HARLAND: *The Obligations of Power: American Diplomacy in the Search for Peace* (New York 1966)
In Washington the author was Assistant Secretary of State for United Nations affairs and in that capacity wielded great influence over the Organisation. His book, which is pleasantly written but in general not notably revealing, reassures its American readers that the Russians in the Secretariat continue to be 'by-passed' in all matters of importance.

DUCHEMIN, JACQUES, TRINQUIER, Colonel et JACQUES LE BAILLY: *Notre Guerre au Katanga* (Paris 1963)
Reflecting the viewpoint of the French O.A.S. 'mercenaries' round Tshombe in 1961. The book is most remarkable for the claim that the death of Secretary-General Dag Hammarskjold at Ndola, Northern Rhodesia, in September 1961, was the result of an attempt, organised by members of this group and other mercenaries on Tshombe's behalf, to 'hi-jack' the Secretary-General's plane with him aboard. Considering the source from which it comes, this assertion deserves more attention and examination than it seems to have received.

EINSTEIN, ALBERT: *On Peace* (ed. O. Nathan and H. Norden, preface by Bertrand Russell: London 1963)
Discussed in text (pp. 297–9). A sense of urgency is not enough, nor is even a great mind, when its real attention is bestowed elsewhere. In his post-war papers on peace and world government, Einstein seems to believe that he is writing in some kind of universal perspective, whereas in fact he writes as a reader of the *New York Times*—probably the best newspaper in the world, but reflecting, like all other newspapers, the views and interests of a particular class in a particular country. Einstein's idea of world government based on world democracy, in our time, is a fine example of the kind of absurdity which results from assuming the American to be the universal. The authority of his name, attached to this absurdity, has been among the barriers to serious investigation of how peace actually is, and how it can be more surely, attained and protected.

EVATT, HERBERT: *Peace on Earth* (New York 1949)
The author was President of the General Assembly at its Third Session (1948). His speeches are remarkable for a blend of idealism and euphoria representative of the early hopes for the United Nations.

FISHER, ROGER (ed.) *International Conflict and Behavioural Science: The Craigville Papers* (New York 1964)
An interesting but disappointing attempt at a combined approach, by scholars of various disciplines. What is astonishing is the lack of attention paid by these scientists to the rich varieties of relevant 'behaviour' going on before their eyes at Turtle Bay.

Follett Vest-Pocket Guide to the United Nations (Chicago 1965)
A useful compendium, with most of the basic documents.

*FOOTE, WILDER (ed): *Servant of Peace: A Selection of the Speeches and Statements of Dag Hammarskjold* (New York and Evanston 1962)
See also 'Hammarskjold'.

FREUD, SIGMUND: *Character and Culture* (New York 1963) the essay 'On War'. This is a 1932 reply to Einstein (see p. 135). Perhaps the most interesting feature of this rather loose and rambling paper is Freud's belief that an institution like the League of Nations, had it existed in 1914, could have averted the First World War. This opinion is not invalidated by the fact that the actual League, a product of the First World War, failed to avert the Second World War, also a product of the First World War.

Civilisation, War and Death (ed. J. Rickman London, 1939)

GRIFFIN, J. EDWARD: *The Fearful Master: A Second Look at the United Nations* (Boston and Los Angeles, 4th printing, 1965)
An American Right Wing view, Birchite or Birchoid.

HALLE, LOUIS J.: *The Cold War as History* (London, 1967)
A useful re-assessment by an American with relevant experience.

*HAMMARSKJOLD, DAG: *Markings* (New York 1964)
Discussed in text (pp. 60–1). See also 'Foote' and 'Lash'

*HILSMAN, ROGER: *To Move a Nation* (New York 1967)
The author was Assistant Secretary of State for Far Eastern Affairs in the Kennedy administration, and had earlier been interested, from an academic point of view, in the politics of foreign policy. In an important chapter 'Military Force and Success' he describes the discussions, at which he was present in the State Department, which led to the decision to back the use of force by the United Nations to end the secession of Katanga.

HOSKYNS, CATHERINE: *The Congo Since Independence* (London 1965)
A scholarly survey which covers the whole period of the United Nations Operation, and contains information not published elsewhere, notably concerning the role played by Secretariat officials in the downfall of the first Prime Minister of the Congo, Patrice Lumumba, and the rise of Mobutu.

*LALL, ARTHUR: *Modern International Negotiation: Principles and Practice* (New York and London 1966)
This book belongs in a very small category, to which Mr Hilsman's book (above) also in part belongs. It is an exhaustive theoretical work by a former official with long and unique experience of practice. The author as Permanent Representative of India was a key figure in the General Assembly in the late fifties, and his knowledge of the workings of the 'parliamentary diplomacy' of the U.N. is probably unrivalled. An excessively scholastic approach renders his book somewhat forbidding—especially in the earlier part—but it repays close reading.

LASH, JOSEPH: *Dag Hammarskjold* (London 1962)
Superficial, but available.

LEFEVER, ERNEST W.: *Ethics and United States Foreign Policy* (New York 1957)
A notable piece of sophisticated philippising. See p. 29.

*LIE, TRYGVE: *In the Cause of Peace* (New York 1954)
Revealing and important (see pp. 124–33). This book remains the only consecutive memoir by a Secretary-General on the period of his tenure.

LORENZ, KONRAD: *On Aggression* (New York, 1966).
Among zoologists, this appears to be a somewhat controversial work. I do not know whether cranes actually behave as Lorenz says they do. If they do, their behaviour is highly relevant to that of diplomats. In any case the relation to human diplomacy of methods of conflict resolution which have been found serviceable in other branches of the animal kingdom clearly merits sustained investigation. See also 'Tiger, Lionel'.

McCLELLAND, CHARLES A. (ed.): *The United Nations: the Continuing Debate* (San Francisco 1960)
A useful anthology of statements representative of various American viewpoints.

MEYER, CORD: *Peace or Anarchy* (Boston 1947)
Discussed in text, p. 253.

MOORE, BERNARD: *The Second Lesson: Seven Years at the United Nations* (London and New York 1957)
Memoirs of a journalist with long experience around both the League and the United Nations: Moderately interesting for the 'tone' of the period described.

NICHOLAS, HERBERT G.: *The United Nations as a Political Institution* (2nd ed. London 1962)
Sensible, but discreet.

SYKES, CHRISTOPHER: *Cross Roads to Israel* (London 1965)
The story of the State of Israel, from its establishment, is fatefully entwined with that of the United Nations. Even before that, in the government of Palestine, the interplay of sacred drama and administrative routine revealed, in an intense and concentrated form, some of the same characteristics as are seen more generally and diffusely at the United Nations. 'Imagination and Government' says the author of this excellent book, 'rarely go together, and this is as well for the partnership as often as not results in deeds of hate and cruelty. But the Palestine administration was in a peculiar situation: *it owed its very existence to an act of imagination,* the Balfour Declaration, *and therefore it could only logically fulfil its function in constantly imaginative action.* It became the task of Palestine administrators on all levels to apply ordinary prosaic administrative methods to the realisation of a poetic dream. This impossibly difficult task was beyond them inevitably.' Italics mine.

**TAVARES DE SA, HERNANE: *The Play Within the Play* (New York 1966)
See pp. 20-2 and *passim*
Exceptionally illuminating: no one else who has been so close to 'the top' of the United Nations for a comparable period has written so candidly about the institution as he knew it.

TIGER, LIONEL: Review-article 'Diplomats, Monkeys and the New Biology' in the *International Journal of the Canadian Institute of International Affairs*, Vol. XXII, No. 1. Winter 1966-7.
Reviewing Lorenz (q.v.) and Ardrey (q.v.) Mr Tiger makes the point: 'Such bizarrely justified horrors as the Viet Nam war urge the thought that if we never learn, is it because we do not know the creature who's learning? Or, to put it the way B. F. Skinner allegedly once did: 'What's in the rat?'

TOYNBEE, ARNOLD: *Change and Habit* (London 1967)
A new summons to World government; see 'Einstein'.

TRAZ, ROBERT DE: *The Spirit of Geneva* (trans. London 1935)
Notable principally for a sardonic and illuminating introduction by Andre Maurois.

VON HORN, GENERAL CARL: *Soldiering for Peace* (London 1966) See p. 33, etc.
Revealing, though not dazzlingly so, about some of the difficulties of peace-keeping.

WALTERS, F. P., *A History of the League of Nations* (London 1952)
Comprehensive, dignified, sad.

WILCOX, FRANCIS O. and H. FIELD HAVILAND (ed.): *The United States and the United Nations* (Baltimore, 1961)
Most of the essays in this are exercises in philippising and the concealment of philippising, but the contribution by Inis L. Claude 'The Containment and Resolution of Disputes' is important.

The present writer's *To Katanga and Back* (London 1962; New York 1963) and the essay 'Conflicting Concepts of the United Nations' in *Writers and Politics*

(London and New York 1965) may also be mentioned; also his article 'The United Nations and the Congo', reviewing C. Hoskyns (above) in *Studies on the Left*, May–June 1966.

(b) SACRED DRAMA

For the mysterious confines where religion, drama and politics meet, the most relevant works are: the plays of Aeschylus and Sophocles; the Bible, especially the Book of Job; the Sixth Book of the *Aeneid*; the *Song of Roland*; the *Divine Comedy*: the plays of Shakespeare, especially *Macbeth* and *Hamlet*; Marlowe's *Dr Faustus*; the plays of Racine especially *Athalie*; *Paradise Lost*, in which the 'great consult' of Pandemonium prefigures and transfigures the United Nations; *Samson Agonistes*; Goethe's *Faust*; the prophetic poems of William Blake; Edmund Burke's *Reflections on the Revolution in France* and *Letters on a Regicide Peace*; Buechner's *Danton's Death*; Carlyle's and Michelet's histories of the French Revolution; the novels of Tolstoy, especially *War and Peace* and *Resurrection*; the novels of Dostoevsky, especially *The Brothers Karamazov* and *The Possessed*; the writings of Nietzsche especially *Thus Spake Zarathustra* and *The Birth of Tragedy*; Hardy's *The Dynasts*; Ibsen's *Brand* and *Peer Gynt*; Kafka's *The Castle* and *The Trial*; the plays of Paul Claudel, especially *L'Otage* and *Le Pain Dur*; Shaw's *Saint Joan*; T. S. Eliot's *Murder in the Cathedral*; W. B. Yeats's poems especially *Meditations in Time of Civil War* and *Cuchulain Comforted* and his plays, especially *Cathleen ni Houlihan*; Thomas Mann's *Dr Faustus*.

The films *Dr Strangelove* and *The War Game* have a special relevance of their own; the whole of the political activity of the United Nations is an attempt to act out an alternative scenario to what these represent.

The following are some other works which I have found relevant either to the whole of these confines or part of them (e.g. politics and literature, politics and religion, religion and literature). The list obviously can have no pretensions to any kind of completeness.

ARDEN, JOHN: *Sergeant Musgrave's Dance* (New York 1960)

Armstrong's Last Goodnight: An exercise in Diplomacy (London 1965)

ARNOLD, THURMAN: *The Folklore of Capitalism* (New Haven and London 1938)
A witty and penetrating pioneering study of the elements of myth and metaphor in various modern institutions. It is sad to see that—if we may judge by some of his recent political pronouncements—the author has himself, in his old age, come to take some of the more extravagant folklore of capitalism at its face value.

BANTON, MICHAEL: *Roles: an Introduction to the Study of Social Relations* (London, 1965)
This important study seems to assume—as do such other 'role-minded' sociological works as I have read—that the *metaphor* of a role is self-evident and stable. Some investigation into the validity of this assumption might prove fruitful.

BENTLEY, ERIC: *Commitments*; two plays performed in New York in 1967: a modern *Antigone* and a modern *Andromaque*, sacred drama on themes of war, peace and race.

The Theatre of Commitment and other Essays on Drama in Our Society (New York 1967)
I received the proofs of this after I had written my text and was struck by certain parallelisms: 'It is all too likely that the artistic impulse—the dramatic impulses particularly—can best find satisfaction today outside the arts altogether.

Here is the drama of science; and even the drama of politics need not be contemptible.' And again: 'A churchman readily understands the power of the theatre because it is a power that resembles his own.'

BRECHT, BERTOLT: *Seven Plays*. Edited and with an introduction by Eric Bentley (New York 1961)
Includes *Saint Joan of the Stockyards*, *Mother Courage* and *Galileo*.

BURKE, KENNETH: *A Grammar of Motives* and *A Rhetoric of Motives* (New York 1962)

CAMUS, ALBERT: *The Fall* (London 1957)

CAUDWELL, CHRISTOPHER: *Illusion and Reality* (London 1937)
Studies in a Dying Culture (London 1938)
Caudwell's idea of 'fantastic reality'—a term which he applies to religion generally—is helpful.

CÉSAIRE, AIMÉ: *Une Saison au Congo* (Paris, 1966)
A play about Lumumba: 'Homme d'imagination . . . homme de foi . . . homme d'Afrique. . . .'

DEUTSCHER, ISAAC: *The Prophet Outcast* (Oxford 1963)
See also Steiner, George.

ELIOT, T. S.: *Notes Towards the Definition of Culture* (London 1948)

EMPSON, WILLIAM: *Seven types of Ambiguity* (London 1930)
Some Versions of Pastoral (London 1935); *Milton's God* (London 1961)

FANON, FRANTZ: *Studies in a Dying Colonialism* (New York 1966)
The treatment of the psychological, social and political significance of the controversy over the *haik* (veiled garment worn by Moslem women) is in itself the narration of a sacred drama. The politico-religious significance of the idea of the veil—'sacred' to Burke, for example—might repay more extensive exploration.

GENET: *The Balcony* (Tr. London 1957); *The Blacks: A Clown Show* (Tr. London 1960); *Our Lady of the Flowers* (Tr. New York 1963); *The Screens* (Tr. London 1963)
No other modern dramatist has such a sense of the importance of ritual. His use of masks—a metaphorical prop as dear to Marxists as the veil is to Burke—is also relevant.

GOLDING, WILLIAM: *Lord of the Flies* (London 1954)
Sacred drama in its sinister aspect.

HARRISON, JANE: *Prolegomena to the Study of Greek Religion* (3rd ed. Cambridge 1922). *Ancient Art and Ritual* (New York 1913)

HOCHHUTH, ROLF: *The Deputy* (New York 1964). Eric Bentley in *The Theory of Commitment* (q.v.) has some valuable comments on this.

HOWARTH, HERBERT: *The Irish Writers, 1880–1940, Literature under Parnell's star* (London 1958). Impact of a political leader on a literary movement.

HUIZINGA: *Homo Ludens: a study of the play element in culture* (London 1949)
My indebtedness to this seminal work is heavy. See especially pp. 275–82.

HYMAN, STANLEY EDGAR: *The Tangled Bank: Darwin, Marx, Frazer and Freud as Imaginative Writers* (New York 1962)
This application of the methods of literary criticism to writings not primarily imaginative is novel and suggestive.

LENIN, V. I. 'Party Organisation and Party Literature', in *Collected Works* (Moscow and London 1960) Vol. VI. A hurried and skimpy paper, but of great consequence.

MAO TSE TUNG: 'Talks to the Yenan Forum' in *Selected Works* Vol III. (Peking 1961)
A much more extended and careful treatment than Lenin's of the relation of literature to the Communist Party.

MARX, KARL: See, in *Karl Marx Early Writings* translated and edicted by T. B. Bottomore (New York 1964), the remarkable commentary on a passage from *Timon of Athens*.
The famous passage about ghosts and Pharaohs at the beginning of *The Eighteenth Brumaire* (1853) is also relevant.

PARKE, H. W. and WORMELL, D. E. W.: *The Delphic Oracle* (2 Vols. Oxford 1956)
I have drawn heavily on this (pp. 245–50) and am happy here to acknowledge my indebtedness to the two distinguished Senior Fellows of Trinity College, Dublin, who are its authors.

RICHARDS, I. A.: *Practical Criticism: a study of literary judgment* (London 1929)
The Screens (London 1961)
Tomorrow Morning, Faustus (London 1962)

SARTRE, J. P.: *Lucifer and the Lord* (trans. of *Le Diable et le Bon Dieu*: (London 1952))

STEINER, GEORGE: *The Death of Tragedy* (London 1961)
Language and Silence (New York 1967)
In the second work there is a stimulating discussion of Trotsky as a tragic hero.

THOMPSON, W. I. M.: *The Imagination of an Insurrection* (New York 1967)
A rather unsatisfactory attempt to deal with an important and difficult theme: the relation of imaginative writing to revolutionary action (in this case the Easter Rising of 1916 in Dublin).

TROTSKY, LEON: *Literature and Revolution* (Ann Arbor Paperback ed. 1960)
The most sustained and sensitive examination of the subject by any leading Marxist.

WEISINGER, HERBERT: *Tragedy and the Paradox of the Fortunate Fall* (London 1953)
The Agony and the Triumph: Papers on the Use and Abuse of Myth (Michigan 1964)

WILSON, EDMUND: *To the Finland Station* (New York 1940)

The following by the present writer, are also relevant:
Maria Cross: Imaginative Patterns in a Group of Catholic Writers (London 1953)
Writers and Politics (London and New York 1965)
'Passion and Cunning': An essay on the Politics of W. B. Yeats': in *In Excited Reverie* (ed. A. N. Jeffares and K. G. W. Cross, London and New York 1965)
'Burke and Marx' in *New American Review*, September 1967
See also the Epilogue to *Parnell and His Party* (Oxford 1957).

BIBLIOGRAPHY II

Bibliography to Appendix 'The Leopard-Skin Priest' by David Brokensha

BOHANNAN, P. J.: *Justice and Judgment among the Tiv* (London: Oxford University Press 1957)

BOHANNAN, PAUL (ed.): *Law and Warfare: Studies in the Anthropology of Conflict* (Garden City, N.Y.: Natural History Press, 1967)
An excellent selection of texts, forming the best single introductory book.

BROKENSHA, DAVID: *Social Change at Larteh, Ghana* (Oxford: Clarendon Press 1966)

EVANS-PRITCHARD, E. E.:
(1) *The Nuer* (Oxford: Clarendon Press, 1940)
(2) *Nuer Religion* (Oxford: Clarendon Press 1956) (especially Chapter XII, 'Priests and Prophets')

EVANS-PRITCHARD, E. E. and FORTES, M. (eds.) *African Political Systems*, (London: Oxford University Press 1940)

GLUCKMAN, MAX:
(1) *The Judicial Process among the Barotse of Northern Rhodesia* (Manchester: Manchester University Press 1955)
(2) *Custom and Conflict in Africa* (Oxford: Basil Blackwell 1956) Vigorous presentation of view that 'conflicts in one set of relationships, over a wider range of society or through a longer period of time, lead to the re-establishment of social cohesion'.
(3) 'Rituals of Rebellion in South-East Africa' in *Order and Rebellion in Tribal Africa*, pp. 110–136 (London, Cohen and West 1963)

GULLIVER, P. H.: *Social Control in an African Society: A Study of the Arusha: Agricultural Masai of Northern Tanganyika* (Boston: Boston University Press 1963)

JAYAWARDENA, CHANDRA: *Conflict and Solidarity in a Guianese Plantation* (London School of Economics, *Monographs on Social Anthropology*, No. 25. London: The Athlone Press 1963)

NADER, LAURA (ed.): *The Ethnography of Law*, American Anthropologist, Vol. 67 No. 6, pt. 2, Dec. 1965. Good overview of main theoretical and methodological problems; excellent bibliographies.

MIDDLETON, JOHN and DAVID TAIT: *Tribes Without Rulers: Studies in African Segmentary Systems* (London: Routledge & Kegan Paul 1958). Especially the section on 'The Exercise of Violence' in Introduction, pp. 19–22.

TURNER, V. W.: *Schism and Continuity in an African Society* (Manchester: Manchester University Press 1957)

TURNER, V. W.: 'Ritual Symbolism, Morality and Social Structure among the Ndembu,' in M. Fortes and G. Dieterlen (ed.) *African Systems of Thought* (London: Oxford University Press 1965)

WILSON, MONICA: *Divine Kings and the 'Breath of Men'* (Cambridge: Cambridge University Press 1959) The Frazer Lecture; a short consideration of anger, unity, and ritual.

ACKNOWLEDGEMENTS

Many friends have helped me with the composition of this book, some of them without knowing that they were doing so. Professor David Grene, of the Committee on Social Thought of the University of Chicago, gave me help of inestimable value, when I first outlined to him the general theme of the book, by indicating to me several works whose relevance to this theme would have been likely to escape me, without the aid of his learning and intuition. Mr. Jonathan Mirsky, of the Department of Chinese, Dartmouth College, Connecticut, brought to bear on the text the resources of an incisive mind, formed by the two great cultures, and of his dedication to the peace movement. His criticisms led me to re-cast entirely both the beginning and the end of the book. Mr David Brokensha, of the Department of Anthropology, University of California, Santa Barbara, signally helped me—at Larteh in Ghana and elsewhere— towards a better understanding of the social functions of religion, ritual and sacred drama; he also, by the example of his own sympathetic alertness, helped to awaken me to the dangers (on my own part) of condescension, in the presence of strange and apparently absurd phenomena. I am still further in his debt for the remarkable Appendix which he has contributed to the present volume.

In Ghana also, Professor I. A. Richards, during an extended stay with us in 1964, suggested, by the forms and quality of his attention to the surrounding political phenomena, the possibilities inherent in an approach to politics quite different from that of either the practical politician or the academic political scientist.

Among those who helped by their conversation, in revealing their specific insights into reality are: my colleagues in the Schweitzer Program at New York University in 1966–7—John Arden, David Caute, George Steiner and Paul Neuberg; other colleagues and friends in New York University and environs, notably James and Rosalind Becker, John Gerassi, Deirdre Levinson, and Leonard and Jean Boudin; members of the American Friends Service Committee at various meetings, gave me the benefit of their serious and undiscouraged thinking on the subject of peace. Professor Herbert Weisinger invited me to talk to his students at Stony Brook about these matters, and encouraged me to persist in this line of enquiry.

Students and others active in the peace movement, and in protests against the war in Vietnam, kept the significance of the sacred drama—mainly in its tragic aspects but a little also in its comic ones—constantly before my mind. Several former colleagues, both in the United Nations Secretariat, in some Delegations and in the Department of External Affairs, helped me in various ways; it is my hope that, in a subsequent edition, if there is one, I may be able to thank them by name. Among the press corps attached, or formerly attached, to the United Nations, I should like to record my indebtedness especially to Andrew Boyd, Bill Fulton and John McNutt.

I am indebted to the authorities of New York University, and in particular to its President, James E. Hester, to the Dean of Washington Square College, William E. Buckler, and to Professor David H. Greene for the congenial conditions of the Schweitzer Program at New York University, highly propitious to a speculative study of this kind, not confined by the walls of any one discipline.

Without Feliks Topolski the book would have been neither written nor drawn; the thought of him drawing the United Nations was the germ of the book itself. When one begins by thinking of the United Nations primarily as a *spectacle* one is led to consider what kind of spectacle it may be.

My wife's welcome for the central idea of the book, her interest in its development, and her criticisms and suggestions, did much to get the book written.

My son, Donal Cruise O'Brien contributed a number of acute and informed criticisms and suggestions as did my daughter-in-law, Rita Cruise O'Brien, and the other persons named in the dedication helped by enlarging the author's concept of relevance and unsettling his assumptions.

Miss Eileen Sheerin, Executive Assistant to the Schweitzer Chair and Mrs Gwen Leen, grappled courageously with a difficult manuscript and helped such order to emerge as has emerged.

I am happy here to record my sincere thanks to all these friends, who have of course no responsibility for such errors and misinterpretations as may have survived their criticisms.

Schweitzer Program
New York University
One Fifth Avenue
New York